At Issue

What Is the Impact of Tourism?

Other Books in the At Issue Series:

At Issue

What Is the Impact of Tourism?

Roman Espejo, Book Editor

GREENHAVEN PRESS

A part of Gale, Cengage Learning

GALE
CENGAGE Learning™

Detroit • New York • San Francisco • New Haven, Conn • Waterville, Maine • London

GALE
CENGAGE Learning™

Christine Nasso, *Publisher*
Elizabeth Des Chenes, *Managing Editor*

© 2009 Greenhaven Press, a part of Gale, Cengage Learning.

Gale and Greenhaven Press are registered trademarks used herein under license.

For more information, contact:
Greenhaven Press
27500 Drake Rd.
Farmington Hills, MI 48331-3535
Or you can visit our Internet site at gale.cengage.com

For product information and technology assistance, contact us at

Gale Customer Support, 1-800-877-4253
For permission to use material from this text or product, submit all requests online at
www.cengage.com/permissions

Further permissions questions can be emailed to permissionrequest@cengage.com

Articles in Greenhaven Press anthologies are often edited for length to meet page requirements. In addition, original titles of these works are changed to clearly present the main thesis and to explicitly indicate the author's opinion. Every effort is made to ensure that Greenhaven Press accurately reflects the original intent of the authors. Every effort has been made to trace the owners of copyrighted material.

Cover photograph © Images.com/Corbis.

LIBRARY OF CONGRESS CATALOGING-IN-PUBLICATION DATA

What is the impact of tourism? / Roman Espejo, book editor.
   p. cm. -- (At issue)
Includes bibliographical references and index.
ISBN 978-0-7377-4120-9 (hardcover)
ISBN 978-0-7377-4121-6 (pbk.)
1. 1. Tourism--Juvenile literature. I. I. Espejo, Roman, 1977-
G155.1.W57 2009
338.4'791--dc22

               2008028524

Printed in the United States of America
1 2 3 4 5 6 7 12 11 10 09 08

Contents

Introduction

Founded in 2004 by Virgin Group chairman Richard Branson, Virgin Galactic offers trips that are, literally, out of this world. With its first commercial flight scheduled for 2009, Virgin Galactic currently books space tours that will take passengers to 62 miles above the earth, enabling them to experience six minutes of weightlessness and take in an unrivaled view of the planet. Its space vehicle prototype, SpaceShipOne, completed three such suborbital space missions. As of May 2008, the self-proclaimed "world's first spaceline" sold almost 200 reservations at a price most vacationers would find astronomical—a ticket for the 2.5 hour flight costs $200,000 and requires a $20,000 deposit.

However, the distinction of being the world's first space tourist belongs to California billionaire Dennis Tito. On April 28, 2001, in Kazakhstan, Tito boarded manned supply mission Soyuz TM-32, spending eight days aboard the International Space Station. A former NASA employee, Tito was turned away from the United States' space program—because he was not a professional astronaut—before he approached the Russian Federal Space Agency with his proposal. After numerous hurdles, Tito acquired the reported $20 million round-trip ticket and accompanied the astronauts on Soyuz TM-32. A year later, South African Mark Shuttleworth became the second nonastronaut to privately fund a space tour through the Russian government, while former 'N Sync member Lance Bass's much-publicized bid to become the first pop star in space failed to launch.

Though it virtually created the market for commercial space travel several years ago, Virgin Galactic already faces competition. XCOR Aerospace, a Californian aerospace company, claims its airplane-sized Lynx rocketplane will be able to perform several suborbital flights a day, starting in 2010. Jeff

Greason, chief executive officer of XCOR, says, "XCOR's mission is to radically lower the cost of spaceflight, because affordable access to space for everyone means far more than breathtaking views and the freedom of weightlessness." EADS (European Aeronautic Defence and Space Company) is also joining the space tourism race. The European aerospace corporation will offer, as early as 2012, suborbital flights similar to Virgin's through its Astrium division.

The unseen hazards, however, paint a tentative future for space tourism. Although the first human flew into space in 1961, scientists are still investigating the effects of space travel on the human body. Some experts warn that more research is needed to assess how exposure to radiation affects passengers on suborbital flights. Furthermore, experiments with monkeys also suggest that small changes in the body's chemistry that occur during space travel may place passengers at heightened risk during medical treatment, such as general anesthesia, back on earth. The hazards also extend to professionals and workers in this early-stage industry. In July 2007, a blast at a space tourism test site in the Mojave desert run by Burt Rutan, designer of Virgin's SpaceShipOne, killed three workers. A rocket motor test in which nitrous oxide flowed through an injector caused the explosion. Though the substance is not known to be dangerous, the site's general manager described activities in the area as "inherently risky."

In addition, when commercial space tourism gets off the ground, some critics anticipate that these tours will pose a challenge to aviation insurance companies. According to Raymond Duffy, vice president at Willis Inspace, "In the beginning, rates are going to be high. They are going to be very high." He explains that "the rates will come way down" when the space tourism industry demonstrates a solid track record for safety, but early failures would make insuring space travel extremely difficult, if impossible. Yet Duffy recommends that the government, except in cases of negligence or misconduct, should not be liable for commercial space flights, as passengers assume the special risks of such travel.

The aerospace industry is also concerned with the potential changes commercial space travel may bring. Some industry professionals argue that space tourists threaten the space programs because they take away scarce seats from professional astronauts and time and opportunities for experiments and research. Observing the growing list of multimillionaires approaching Russia for space tours, a Russian aerospace official states, "It's time to stop flying to space 'just for flying.'"

Space is still a highly exclusive destination of the thrill-seeking and very rich select few. Nonetheless, noted aerospace expert Patrick Collins predicted in his 2000 presentation, "The Space Tourism Industry in 2030," that the industry will thrive, and space travel will ultimately become accessible. Collins projects that space flight prices will drop to $25,000 by 2017, and the number of commercial space passengers will reach 1 million a year by 2020. If Collins's predictions are accurate, space tourism will have profound implications not only for the travel industry, but for the human race and the planet. But modern-day tourism, without the prospect of commercial space travel, already produces social, economic, and environmental changes on a global scale. These changes are topics of critical inquiry in *At Issue: What Is the Impact of Tourism?*

1

The Tourism Industry Is Responsive to the Negative Impacts of Tourism

Dan Luzadder

Dan Luzadder is a reporter for Travel Weekly.

Because of mounting concerns over global warming, pollution, and energy consumption, sustainability is becoming key to the tourism industry. For instance, industry leaders are encouraging more transparency and accountability, such as providing environmental ratings for hotels and increasing consumer awareness of travel and leisure companies' green interests and practices. In addition, rental car franchises and airlines are seeking to reduce their emissions, and hotel chains are employing technologies that reduce the consumption of resources. Environmental responsibility, therefore, is very much a part of the tourism industry's agenda.

"I decided to take a walk on the beach, and I saw four young Bangladeshi men struggling to drag a portable air-conditioning contraption to a beach shack. It was a heavy, metal box, trailing all sorts of electrical wires in the sand behind it."

The man relating this unlikely scene was Chris Luebkeman, director of Global Foresight and Innovation for the U.K.-based Arup Group. He was talking by cell phone from his hotel room in Dubai.

Dan Luzadder, "Seeding Responsible Tourism," *Travel Weekly*, vol. 66, May 7, 2007, pp. 18–25. Copyright © 2007 NorthStar Travel Media, LLC. Reproduced by permission.

The workers, he said, were from a nearby hotel and were trying to bring a little cool comfort to a handful of tourists spending their afternoon on blistering sand. The sight of it "may just have been one of the most ridiculous things I have ever seen."

The very idea of cooling a beach cabana . . . with expensive, portable air conditioners . . . flies in the face of what is fast becoming the agenda of responsible environmental behavior for tourism providers.

Luebkeman's job is to peer into the unsettled future by studying details of the present-day world. And in the contrast between the commonplace and the unusual—even in things that appear ludicrous—he seeks inspiration for change. The very idea of cooling a beach cabana in one of the world's hottest climates with expensive, portable air conditioners, particularly in these days of hyper-awareness regarding carbon emissions, flies in the face of what is fast becoming the agenda of responsible environmental behavior for tourism providers.

The incident that Luebkeman observed is one example of increasing dissonance between the boom in travel worldwide and global environmental concerns. It is also emblematic of the issues being confronted this week by industry leaders at the 2007 World Travel and Tourism Council's [WTTC] Global Travel and Tourism Summit in Lisbon.

The WTTC, whose 97 dues-paying members include the CEOs [chief executive officers] of the world's largest travel companies (think American Express, Starwood, TUI, Marriott, Carlson), meets annually to discuss pressing industry concerns. And as the world is poised to anoint travel the cultural common denominator of the planet (it now accounts for some 10% of the global gross domestic product and employs more than 231 million people worldwide), the question of just what is appropriate business behavior in the age of global warming has jumped to the top of the agenda. The theme of the summit is "Breaking Barriers and Managing Growth."

With leisure tourism projected to grow 4.2% annually over the next decade, and with an emerging middle class in China and India preparing to inject hundreds of millions of travelers into the infrastructure of world tourism, environmental and social challenges are already reaching critical mass. The WTTC Summit is drawing, in addition to its own membership, hundreds of interested parties to join in the discussion about how to plan for future travel and tourism responsibly.

In the weeks leading up to the summit, Travel Weekly conducted a series of interviews with top tourism industry leaders—some WTTC members, some not—as they prepared to head to Lisbon. It became amply clear during those discussions that both awareness of climate change and the use of human capital are driving new decisions and new perspectives on balancing sound commercial judgment with social responsibility.

On the whole, industry leaders say they are convinced that the journey of discovery they are now taking will lead to new ideas and a better understanding of how to balance environmental and social challenges with one of the most favorable economic opportunities the industry has ever enjoyed.

"We have a situation which, I must say, I haven't seen in my 42 years of activity in this crazy industry," said Jean Claude Baumgarten, president of the WTTC. "Things are doing fine all over the world. Traffic is growing, . . . which is fantastic. And it seems like the goodies are equally spread all over the world.

"So that creates on one side good feelings. But growth creates new challenges. It creates new types of priorities."

Amid the backdrop of the vital contributions world travel can make to cultural interaction, to understanding and to international stability, voices like Luebkeman's warn that if the industry doesn't take steps to build with environmentally sound designs that help reduce energy consumption, waste and other problems that add to its carbon footprint, then pressure from outside, in the form of government regulation and taxes, may do it for them. (Luebkeman will be moderating a session at the summit.)

Andrew Cosslett, CEO of InterContinental Hotels Group [IHG], said he would making his first trip to a WTTC Summit and was approaching it with high expectations.

"We certainly start with a view that says, on the [whole] the travel industry is a good thing in the world," Cosslett said. "There is no question that the demand factors are very powerful and that notwithstanding any concerns around environmental issues, there will be strong tailwinds pushing growth in the travel market for the next decade. There are tremendous drivers here, and it is a positive thing to bring people in the world together.

"But the question is: How can you make a consistent impact for the good? I think our business is trying to begin the process of understanding what more we can do in that area."

For many, the discussions at the summit, which will be held as a forum in the round, are a starting point in what, until now, have been isolated commitments to environmental responsibility by corporations.

I think as an industry, we are starting to wake up.

At Fairmont Hotels and Resorts, that commitment started nearly two decades ago, with environmental awareness followed by specific actions. Michelle White, Fairmont's director of environmental affairs, said she saw the gathering as a milestone in the evolution of a more responsible tourism industry.

"Environmental awareness . . . is on the upswing in the industry," White said. "A lot of organizations have a lot of work to do. But the environment is not a destination, it is a journey, so there is always something to do. I think as an industry, we are starting to wake up.

"So just having this particular summit and having these people in one room discussing these issues is significant because these are the decision-makers."

That point was echoed by others preparing to attend the event as well as by outside observers. The influence of chief executives and other industry leaders participating in the discussions (*Travel Weekly*'s editor in chief, Arnie Weissmann, is a speaker at the summit) is not only important, they say, but will bring candor to the discussions, even between those who compete with each other on a daily basis.

"CEOs are also individuals," Baumgarten said. "The CEO of an organization has to put his personal conviction in sync with the daily job. I think we have more CEOs who are deeply convinced that this is the right thing to do. And the combination of the two will bring more candid dialogue than [skeptics] might consider."

Some of those CEOs are putting their money behind their convictions. The group includes Jeff Clarke, the CEO of Travelport, which owns Orbitz and Galileo. Travelport has pledged to buy the carbon offsets to cover the carbon emissions generated by the travel of industry and public sector leaders to the WTTC Summit.

Travelport has made other contributions, as well, Clarke said, particularly in promoting transparency in the industry. He said his company was providing or planning to provide environmental ratings for hotels and other suppliers to enable consumers to see the environmental interests of those they might do business with and to exert their own influence, via spending choices, on environmental and corporate responsibility.

"This is on the mind of every CEO in the industry," Clarke said. "It is not only on our minds because of responsibility, but also because it is a personal interest, a personal interest of mine and many other CEOs.

"I don't think there is any debate any longer on the impact of carbon on world temperatures," he continued. "There is no question: The scientific evidence is in, and now is the time when the industry needs to react to this.

"One of the things we at Travelport can do as an intermediary, as technology providers, is to measure travel: We have the ability to do that. There are 800,000 bookings a day. We know where the destinations are. And we are considering initiatives to start building improved transparency by setting up travel indexes that let consumers and environmental organizations know the extent of travel."

Travelport has also created a partnership with the nonprofit Carbon Fund to help consumers voluntarily pay to offset carbon emissions that result from travel. Capital raised in that process is being used to fund energy production from wind, waves, solar and co-generation projects. It is also being used to plant trees, which remove carbon dioxide from the air and replenish oxygen through photosynthesis.

While the airline industry is often singled out as a major source of carbon emissions, there are other sources of travel-related emissions that rank higher, including cars and other ground transportation.

In the car rental industry, some companies are acknowledging that reality by offering hybrids and alternative-fuel vehicles for customers who want a more environmentally friendly ride.

Luebkeman notes that only 3% to 4% of greenhouse gases are traceable to aircraft. Nonetheless, the perception that planes are a major source of emissions has motivated companies like Natural Air, a small airline based in Costa Rica, to become carbon neutral.

To do that, Natural Air has focused on finding alternative fuels, as has been proposed by Virgin Atlantic's Richard Branson, but on carbon offsets that include company efforts to plant enough trees in Costa Rica's forests to account for the carbon that the airline's operations put into the atmosphere.

Hotel chains say they have long taken steps to design and build properties to make them more energy efficient.

Environmentalists say, however, that while airline emissions are very much on the public's mind, hotels and other buildings related to tourism infrastructure are potentially a greater source of environmental pollution.

Hotel chains say they have long taken steps to design and build properties to make them more energy efficient. And they point to initiatives with customers to reduce water usage and linen usage as a way to reduce their environmental impact.

Ed Fuller, president and managing director of international lodging at Marriott International, said the lodging industry had made other major steps over the past few years to improve its environmental status. But he acknowledged that there was more to do.

"There are other parts of the industry that could be more conscious and aware of the issues," he said, "and things like the summit will give people the feeling that there is effort under way. I think cooperation and the opportunity to talk about it is very positive.

"When you get right down to it, the world is ready to try to turn this situation around," he continued. "Yet people also want to be able to take advantage of travel and use those opportunities to have a better understanding of the world around them."

Arthur de Haast, Global CEO for Jones Lang LaSalle Hotels, said: "It's in the best interests of the travel and tourism industry to take the issues of environmental sustainability and corporate social responsibility seriously. The WTTC Summit is an excellent opportunity for the world's most influential companies to address them in a comprehensive and coordinated manner."

Jabulani Mabuza, CEO of Tsogo Sun Holdings in South Africa, which operates casinos and accommodations, said corporate responsibility was close to his company's heart.

"In China, India, Africa, the culture has changed," Mabuza said. "Here, black people [were] migrant providers of labor, and so they never traveled their own country. Now, those who have started to travel their own country want to travel outside it.

"So the question is: Are there conditions in place for this growth to be shared with the whole of the larger community?" he said. "Will it present prosperity for all, or will this opportunity for growth be consumed by the various tensions? Are we as businesspeople going to be deluded by our own greed for profit? Or are we going to say that world travel and tourism as a sector is capable to act as a responsible corporate citizen? Are we going to be able to balance the need of all our stakeholders, be it commercial, social [or] cultural?"

As consumers themselves turn to decision-making based on environmentally friendly and socially conscious criteria, the heightened awareness of the need to take care of the planet has already become a higher priority in the industry, just as environmental issues are commanding greater attention within other major industries.

Such discussions are coming, say industry leaders, at a time when the road taken leads either to sustainable growth and lives in developing [countries] and developed or to destruction of the planet's environment.

Erika Harms, director of sustainable development for the United Nations Foundation, which is active in protecting World Heritage sites, said the travel industry, as is true with industrial concerns across the board, appears to be at a tipping point.

"Things could go either way," she said. "What we are seeing is there is a broader understanding from the industry, be it driven by consumers or competition, that business as usual is not the way to go. That is pretty new. The original trend and what has been around for 20 years is the ecotourism components. But that is just a small niche that does not address the broader issues of mass tourism. It is in mass tourism where there is recognition that there needs to be a change. There are leaders and followers and those who never change."

On the other hand, Harms said, "There is also less apprehension by the industry to talk about sustainable tourism now. Many of those in the industry still do it in the wrong way because sustainable tourism does not equate to ecotourism. There is a need to educate travelers and the industry about that."

The litany of tourism sites where short-term, profit-driven behavior has had devastating consequences is long. Ignoring pollution, exploiting low-cost labor and development in sensitive areas has damaged many local communities.

For example, at the beaches of Pattaya in Thailand, swimming has long been discouraged because of wastewater pollution. The consequences for the failure to keep the local community clean and vibrant are long lasting and have an economic impact. The story is the same at many points along the Thai coast at beaches that were once among the most beautiful in the world.

But the counterpoint can be seen in places like the Inter-Continental Bora Bora Resort and Thalasso Spa, where new technology provides air conditioning to resort guests in a low-energy, cost-effective way.

"It is quite intriguing," Cosslett said. "We have massively reduced the electricity consumption there by 90%, and we did this with a creative and innovative system by putting in the world's deepest underwater pipeline. Bora Bora sits on a deep trench line in the ocean, and a pipeline goes down to 6,000 feet into ultracool water, which is pumped to the surface to cool the island's resort.

"It's been done before in homes, but this is the first time it has been done with ocean water," he said. "It is one resort making a difference, and, especially in places like Bora Bora, it is important to show leadership."

Another company that has committed to environmental leadership is Six Senses Resorts and Spas, which is headquartered in Bangkok and operates out of Thailand, the Maldives and Vietnam.

Chairman and CEO Sonu Shivdasani, who owns the luxury resort company with his wife, Eva Malmstrom Shivdasani, has set a tone of investment in a future built on environmentally sound practices, conservation and use of innovative technology.

"There comes a point where what you're doing has to do more than just generate income," Shivdasani said. "We are trying to create enriching experiences in a sustainable environment. That is ingrained in us. My wife is a big environmentalist, and we follow her to an extent. It is so difficult to get up every morning and go to work thinking you are putting the environment on a path to extinction."

He said that at one of the resorts where the company was a majority owner, they set a goal of zero emissions by 2010, and were on their way to meeting those expectations, having cut carbon emissions by half since the project started last year [2006]. The resort is carbon neutral now, having offset the rest of emissions through a U.K.-based nonprofit, the Converging World.

Shivdasani is also investing in a chilling system similar to the one IHG is using in Bora Bora as well as natural laundry drying, recirculating hot water and other energy technology that will allow for the cost of zero-emissions status to be recovered within nine years, given the current high cost of nonrenewable fuels.

[People] don't have to go backpacking to have a low impact on the environment but can find luxury tourism that is sustainable and not destructive.

Using green building techniques has also reduced the cost of air conditioning in his Maldives resorts and elsewhere in their 1,500-employee Asian operations, he said. They are also exploring an "ecosuite" that would be self-sufficient.

In the process, he says, the company is conveying to people that they don't have to go backpacking to have a low impact on the environment but can find luxury tourism that is sustainable and not destructive.

The expense of investing in such policies often results in overall cost savings, a point that Luebkeman is fond of making.

"This is no longer a case of the fringe doing things," says Luebkeman. "What we are seeing now is major CEOs around the world realizing that they need to do something. And the clever ones actually see this as a way to save money."

Luebkeman cited as an example a village in northern England, Ashton Hayes, which started a grassroots movement to become the first town to be carbon neutral.

In the process, a reluctant participant, a pub owner, was persuaded by the results of a survey by a local university to turn his restaurant grills on later in the day, unplug equipment not being used and employ other ways to reduce energy consumption.

"The result was he saved $5,000 a month in expenses, $60,000 a year," said Luebkeman, "just from changing the patterns of how he was running his pub. Now he is the biggest vocal supporter of the movement, not as an ultra-greenie, not because it helped the world, but because it helped him. He has started to look at where the food comes from for his restaurants, the carbon cost of shipping, and is patronizing local providers, things like that."

It is an idea that has particular appeal for others in the travel and tourism segments, particularly within corporate social responsibility movements, among which using local services, local labor and other interests that benefit local communities is gathering momentum around the globe.

With growing prosperity in China and elsewhere in Asia and the resultant increase in desire among the new middle class to see the world and experience other cultures, the infrastructure of the industry will soon experience more pressure to accommodate a huge growth in travelers.

And with that comes the need for capital. Wise use of capital, both in terms of monetary investment and bringing economic benefits to local communities and individuals (as well as distant corporations), is expected to bring increased scrutiny to the agenda of the industry and its interaction with nations, local governments, nongovernmental organizations and nonprofits.

Many of the industry leaders interviewed for this story said that failure by the industry to respond to concerns about the environment would clearly lead government to step in with regulation of travel and imposition of taxes to help mitigate potential environmental impacts. None saw that as a favorable result.

Robert Darbelnet, CEO of AAA [American Automobile Association], said that educating corporate leaders in sound practices was important for the industry. But just as important, he said, is the industry's responsibility to educate the public and the public sector in what it is doing to facilitate responsible travel and tourism.

As governments consider regulations that could include restrictions on travel (for security as well as environmental reasons), Darbelnet said he believed it was important to get out the message that the industry is taking all its responsibilities seriously.

But he said he did not believe the environment would stand in isolation as the only issue in need of being immediately addressed.

"The environmental issues may have more sizzle right now and may lend themselves appropriately to this level of debate, but there are other issues related to security and the reasonably free passage of people across borders that are also critical in allowing the industry to develop its complete potential," Darbelnet said. "We can't sit on the sidelines. There might be some agreement [at the summit] that we need to advance these issues as well."

2

The Tourism Industry Is Not Responsive to the Negative Impacts of Tourism

Richard Hammond

Richard Hammond writes a monthly column in The Guardian *on eco-friendly holidays.*

In the following viewpoint, Richard Hammond explains that even though the market for eco-friendly tourism is growing, tourism is still destructive to the environment and indigenous cultures. Hammond explains that air travel produces a huge amount of carbon dioxide emissions, which contributes to climate change. Even though tourism dollars can help non-industrialized countries, those dollars rarely reach locals. Indigenous culture and the environment can suffer from irresponsible travelers, but Hammond provides a list of ways to offset the negative impacts of tourism. It is still possible, he concludes, to travel responsibly. One just must be educated and conscientious.

This summer millions of us will take to the skies for our annual holiday, to rest and recharge. According to the World Tourism Organization, we're increasingly choosing greener holidays, from organic farm-stay breaks in Donegal to township tourism tours in Port Elizabeth. The market for 'responsible travel' is growing at a healthy 3–5%, and as the travelling public wakes up to greener living, responsible travel seemingly has the whole world at its feet.

Richard Hammond, "All Aboard the Skylark!" *Resurgence*, May/June 2005. Reproduced by permission.

Air Pollution

Yet paradoxically, in seeking greener holidays in far-flung places, we are jumping more on planes that produce polluting greenhouse gases and contribute to climate change. According to Future Forests, the amount of carbon dioxide an average car emits in an entire year is less than that produced from one return flight to Australia (approximately 3.74 tonnes).

Climate change is now as high up on the global agenda as poverty and terrorism, so how can any travel—green or otherwise—that involves flying be called responsible?

That's one seat on one plane. Even if you only take short-haul flights from the UK to Europe, putting that in a global context is a frightening statistic: the International Air Transport Association recorded 1.8 billion air passenger trips in 2003. The United Nations Intergovernmental Panel on Climate Change (IPCC) says that aviation is the single largest contributor to greenhouse gases (currently about 3.5 per cent), which it says is likely to rise to 15 per cent by the year 2050 if the growth of aviation continues unchecked. Climate change is now as high up on the global agenda as poverty and terrorism, so how can any travel—green or otherwise—that involves flying be called responsible?

According to Justin Francis, managing director of online travel agency responsibletravel.com, "You have to look at the overall picture; not just the flight in isolation, but also what happens as a result of your holiday." Tourism, he says, provides many benefits to destination economies, especially in the non-industrialised countries. Fourteen of the top twenty long-haul destinations are now in these countries, and visitor numbers to many of these countries have doubled, or even tripled, in the last decade. So it's not surprising that tourism has become the main money-earner for a third of non-industrialised countries.

Not All Tourism Dollars Reach Locals

According to Francis, British tourists spend £2 billion a year in non-industrialised countries, "the same amount that the UK Government allocates for its aid budget". While he admits not all of tourists' money reaches local people, a significant amount does, which, he says, is more than what they would get if tourism were abandoned in favour of alternative industries—for instance, mining or logging.

It's not just economic benefits that tourism brings to non-industrialised countries; there are cultural and environmental spin-offs that tourism generates worldwide. The World Wide Fund for Nature's stance on tourism is that the environmental consequences of flying should be considered as part of an overall sustainable strategy that takes into account not only the economic contribution tourism can bring to destinations, but also the social, cultural, and even environmental benefits.

UNESCO's World Heritage List contains 788 'honeypot' sites, including Australia's Barrier Reef and the Acropolis in Athens, magnets for millions of tourists each year whose money helps contribute to the conservation of these sites of natural and cultural significance. Vast areas of wilderness are now protected as parks or reserves, many of which are largely supported by tourism revenues and would struggle to survive without them. Travel also broadens the mind, provides inspiration to millions of young globetrotters, and plays an invaluable role as a global vehicle for promoting the understanding and appreciation of different cultures.

Climate Change

Yet for all tourism's economic, social and environmental benefits, philanthropic and inclusive, it doesn't sit comfortably with the environmental consequences of climate change, given the enormous potential damage it is predicted to inflict on some of the most fragile places, many of which are the very places we wish to visit on holiday. Many of the low-lying islands in the Maldives could disappear in as little as thirty years' time, and coral reefs are already suffering from coral bleaching. Moreover, climate change is likely to threaten the viability of life in many of the world's most vulnerable and poverty-stricken regions—many of which Westerners are unlikely to visit, as they aren't tourist destinations.

What, then, are we to do? Should we all just stay at home, tucked up in energy-efficient cocoons, and pore over holiday brochures of places that are within walking distance? It is clear that the culture of tourism and long-distance travel is firmly entrenched, so we need to make it more responsible—both ethically and environmentally. (See box of 'Tips for Responsible Travel'.)

There is a growing number of environmental organisations that help travellers offset the carbon that is produced from their holiday flights. Future Forests www.futureforests.com, Friends of Conservation www.foc-uk.com and Climate Care www.climatecare.org provide tools on their websites to work out how much money is needed to support the development of renewable and clean energy projects that can offset the share of the pollution generated from a flight. A return flight to Sydney, for example, would set you back £30; a return flight to Madrid, just £5.

The contribution of the aviation industry to greenhouse-gas emissions has to be tackled head on if tourism is to stand any chance of gaining credibility as a responsible industry.

Aviation Fuel Tax

Carbon offsetting at this individual level has credible aims, but it doesn't tackle the root of the problem. According to Dr David Viner at the Climatic Research Unit at the University of East Anglia, the most effective way to tackle aviation's contribution to greenhouse gases is by reducing the use of aviation in general—for example, by implementing an aviation fuel tax. It is likely that a tax will eventually come into legislation, but in the meantime more immediate action is needed, such as carbon trading between airlines, which would at least stem the uncontained increase in emissions.

Viner proposes that we change the way we view flying, seeing it for its true environmental cost rather than as an increasingly cheap and fast way to travel. By balancing out a long-haul holiday with more environmentally sound travel for the rest of the year, or mixing up long-distance trips with holidays closer to home, we could significantly reduce our 'carbon debt'.

Hugh Somerville, ex-head of British Airways' Sustainable Business Unit, says the leading airlines are now addressing the problem of carbon emissions, and the UK aviation industry is trying to join the European Carbon Emissions Scheme by 2008. However, he says the barrier to all of this is the global context, as "there are fears the American carriers might object to such a scheme on the basis of their European operations."

Tourism undoubtedly provides financial and other tangible benefits to holiday destinations, and more responsible tourism makes a significant impact on lessening the ills of tourism's global stampede. However, the contribution of the aviation industry to greenhouse-gas emissions has to be tackled head on if tourism is to stand any chance of gaining credibility as a responsible industry. Aviation fuel tax and carbon trading are unlikely to happen overnight, so the changes that travellers make at the individual level are important in the face of the rapidly growing aviation industry. But unless significant improvements are made to reduce aviation's ecological footprint, the responsible tourism movement will continue to be a worthy yet optimistic patter amid the deafening roar of an increasingly polluting industry, the consequences of which for climate change are becoming all too apparent.

Tips for Responsible Travel

- Read up on the countries you plan to visit and learn even a few words of the local language.

- Help the local economy by buying local produce in preference to imported goods.

- Have respect for local cultures, traditions and holy places. Ask permission before you photograph local people, and always dress appropriately.

- Use water sparingly—local people may not have sufficient clean water.

- Use public transport, hire a bike or walk—you'll meet local people and get to know the place better.

- Don't buy products made from endangered species or hard woods, shells from beach traders, or ancient artefacts.

- Think about where your money goes—for example, B&Bs, village houses and locally owned accommodation benefit local families.

- Pack small gifts from home for your hosts.

3

Tourism Contributes to Economic Growth

Stephan Gross and Jurgen Ringbeck

Senior associate Stephan Gross and senior vice president Jurgen
Ringbeck work for Booz Allen Hamilton, a German-based management consulting firm.

*The travel and tourism industry stimulates economic growth by
increasing national wealth, fostering trade, creating jobs, and
raising wages. In fact, the industry generates income at an annual growth rate of 11 percent, surpassing the worldwide
economy. Therefore, developing nations should capitalize on
travel and tourism by creating safe, stable political climates;
maintaining infrastructures that support transportation and rec-
reation; and deregulating and privatizing domestic industries.
Also, it is recommended that industrialized nations look to the
booming travel and tourism industry as a source of wealth while
seeking innovation and sustainability.*

What does it take for a country's economic growth to
outpace its peers? A strong manufacturing sector? A
productive labor force? Plenty of disposable income? Probably.
But here's a somewhat unexpected answer: a strong travel and
tourism (T&T) industry. That was the primary conclusion
reached by Booz Allen Hamilton's Travel and Tourism Competitiveness Report 2007, which was jointly developed with
the World Economic Forum and other leading organizations
and operators in the industry.

Over the past 50 years, international tourism has increased at an average of 6.5 percent per year, growing from less than 25 million travelers in the 1950s to more than 800 million today.

Many countries have recognized travel and tourism as a critical sector that can incubate national prosperity and economic growth.

According to the World Travel Organization [UNWTO], the income generated from T&T increased at an even greater rate during the same period, reaching 11 percent growth per year and outpacing the world economy. Today, global revenue from travel and tourism exceeds many other major export categories, such as food products and textiles. As tourism has become one of the major industries in international commerce, it has become a major income source, especially for many developing countries. Yet as globalization moves the world closer together, global tourism becomes increasingly diversified as competition among destinations gets fiercer. In the 1950s, the top 15 destinations took up 97 percent of international arrivals; today, those destinations account for only 58 percent.

With T&T income growing, many countries have recognized travel and tourism as a critical sector that can incubate national prosperity and economic growth. But how?

To give governments, T&T operators, and investors a better understanding of the factors that drive the sector's competitiveness, we undertook a cross-country analysis of comparative qualitative and quantitative information—providing a platform for dialogue between industry and policymakers worldwide to address the obstacles to T&T competitiveness.

Evaluating and ranking T&T industries in 124 countries around the globe, the study identifies "best practice" countries that leverage the sector's potential by using it as an incubator for economic growth and social welfare. From top-rated Switzerland all the way down to Chad, we have analyzed more than 50 different variables—including statutory regulatory framework, health and safety, infrastructure, local price levels, and aspects of environment and culture—that impact a country's potential for developing travel and tourism. We found a high correlation—about 80 percent—between the index results and countries' GDP growth development, indicating that the travel sector is a major contributor to economic welfare. As globalization shrinks the world, T&T has clearly become an important means of stimulating local development, accelerating local investment, and boosting employment and public education.

Drivers of T&T Competitiveness

By analyzing the best performers in the T&T index, we also identified the elements that countries need to consider to build a thriving travel and tourism industry. A stable and relatively *risk-free political and regulatory environment* was reconfirmed as a prerequisite of a high-performing T&T sector. This environment includes a high degree of safety and security, good health, hygienic and environmental standards, and liberal economic policies. As the global business community is averse to risky business conditions, political and economic stability is absolutely essential for attracting private capital, foreign investors, and international business travelers and tourists. We also found that every country with a fast-growth travel sector encourages foreign and private ownership, direct investments, property rights, and technological innovation. Indeed, the right regulatory framework is crucial to a country's success: We found that it influenced the competitiveness of the T&T sector the most (with a 97 percent correlation).

Almost as important (showing a 96 percent correlation) is *business infrastructure*: whether a country has succeeded in putting together the type of air, ground, and tourism networks—created through direct government investment, state subsidies, or by entering into public–private partnerships— that will attract both visitors and private investors; whether there are enough quality hotels and banks to meet the needs of travelers; and whether a country's information and communications technology—from broadband access to cell-phone coverage to e-booking and electronic payment services—can adequately meet the needs of the 21st-century business traveler and tourist.

In a globalizing world, the unique value of tourism to emerging markets is easy to see.

If supported by open domestic market conditions fostered by a focused and well-balanced political and regulatory approach, travel and tourism can provide promising economic opportunities in many countries, especially among developing economies, many of which have already started to realize this potential. Over the past ten years alone, developing economies' market share of international arrivals grew from 28.6 percent to 40.3 percent. The UNWTO estimates that up to 40 percent of small economies' GDP and jobs can be generated by T&T. Over the past decade, tourism in the world's 49 poorest countries grew at a rate six times faster than in Europe and the United States. In fact, tourism increased at a rate of 6–8 percent a year collectively in China, India, Africa, and the Middle East, compared with 3–5 percent growth in Europe and the United States. In a globalizing world, the unique value of tourism to emerging markets is easy to see.

Because developing countries have limited sources of income and access to foreign capital, they often struggle to develop their industries and trade. Many such countries, like Turkey or Egypt, are proof that investment in travel and tourism can become an important incubator for national economies, contributing to overall development in several ways:

- Money raised through the T&T sector can be invested in other sectors.

- Upgrades necessary for T&T also benefit citizens and the domestic business environment.

- Domestic workers in the T&T sector can further develop their skills and act as role models, promoting advanced education among all citizens.

- Growth in the T&T industry will generate spillover effects in other markets (e.g., by attracting foreign investors).

Steps to Improve Travel and Tourism

Successfully building a highly competitive T&T sector requires several evolutionary steps. Governments must first make sure an appropriate infrastructure capacity and a basic national operator structure are in place to provide access for domestic and international travelers. Preferably they do so by pulling in international capabilities (e.g., engineering and construction firms as well as consultants) and leveraging private capital early in the process through such strategies as public–private partnerships. Both public regulators and private investors need to ensure that, by focusing on the demand characteristics of their markets, they jointly manage such partnerships efficiently.

Once basic infrastructure is in place, governments must ensure that service operators match growing market demand and increase their performance in both service quality and quantity (e.g., by increasing hotel capacity, number of routes and destinations served, and frequency of flights). To increase performance of the T&T sector itself, governments should engage in further deregulation and privatization, providing a platform for further demand stimulation and growth. Following deregulation of domestic entities—hotels, ground operators, air operators, etc.—cross-border liberalization of a whole region's policy framework can effectively attract new market entrants and improve the industry's overall performance. That in turn can drive down both prices and costs, while stimulating service quality and demand across all T&T players in the region.

While emerging and developing countries are at the beginning of these evolutionary steps toward T&T competitiveness, industrialized countries are typically farther along. Due to well-developed infrastructures, assured statutory framework conditions, and high levels of education, industrialized nations rank higher overall in the T&T index. For example, only five of the top 20 countries are outside Europe and North America. Top performers within industrialized economies, like No. 1-ranked Switzerland, score high by virtue of innovative and sustainable T&T strategies, careful preservation of their attractive natural assets. and high prioritization of the industry on the government's agenda. Even for some of the industrialized countries, T&T is a lead sector, contributing a significant part of the overall wealth of the country. In Switzerland, T&T accounts for 6.2 percent of the GDP; in Spain, 6.6 percent; in France, 4.2 percent. However, even countries like Germany and the United States, which are less dependent on T&T as a core source of income have an increasing incentive to strengthen the competitiveness of their sector and develop it into a broader source of income and wealth.

A New Source of Wealth

In a world where international travel continues to grow, international T&T presents an increasingly attractive business opportunity. Industrialized countries that put a high priority on T&T are able to exploit a new source of wealth that might well substitute for shrinking traditional industries driven by global trends like offshoring or global sourcing and production that play to the favor of emerging regions. While U.S. and European citizens did exploit the Asian markets as travelers in the second half of 20th century, the next decade will be characterized by a growing number of wealthy Asian and Middle Eastern travelers who consider Europe or the United States as a preferred holiday destination. Industrialized nations that accommodate the requirements of these new tourists in service offerings and quality will get the most out of this emerging opportunity.

[Tourism] increases trade, advances development, and creates higher disposable incomes.

So how can industrialized regions with highly developed infrastructures and privatized national T&T sectors rise to the next level and further improve their competitiveness? A sig nificant part of the answer is to continue to privatize and deregulate the sector and to open up travel segments even more for international competition. For example, as a consequence of cross-border European air markets opening up and low-cost carriers entering, average flight prices have fallen by up to 18 percent over the past five years. This stimulated overall European expenditure on travel above the normal levels of growth—by an additional 13 percent, or 82 million passengers. But there is still room for improvement; for example, the largest air travel market between Europe and the United States is still somewhat limited by historic bilateral air-services agreements that restricted numbers of airlines and flights, as well as the destinations that may be served. These restrictions have held back growth in the world's most important international air travel market: the North Atlantic. Booz Allen Hamilton determined in a study for the European Commission that a fully "open aviation area" (OAA) between the United States and the European Union would result in new routes and new market entrants, generating 26 million additional passengers over five years. Economic benefits from the removal of the constraints, quantified in the form of a consumer surplus, would be worth between €6.4 billion and €12 billion over the five-year period. As additional demand would require additional resources, 72,000 new jobs across the European Union and the United States could be expected within that same period.

The Backbone of Globalization

International travel and tourism is the backbone of globalization and enriches the world in many ways: It promotes economic growth, increases trade, advances development, and creates higher disposable incomes. It also strengthens communities, and, by bringing together people from diverse regions and backgrounds, advances the goals of peace and global understanding. These benefits hold true for developing, emerging, and industrialized countries, and they provide a major platform on which other industries can build. Prioritizing the sector and defining a strategic agenda around high-quality, innovative, and sustainable solutions that stimulate both in- and outbound travel are the keys to unleashing the T&T sector's full potential. To succeed, governments must develop a clear vision, commit to engaging all stakeholders in the process, and make a determined effort to work hand in hand with the private travel and tourism sector.

4

Tourism Can Have Negative Economic Consequences

UNEP (United Nations Environment Programme) Tourism Programme

UNEP [United Nations Environment Programme] Tourism Programme is the service branch established by the United Nations that addresses the social, economic, and environmental issues of tourism.

The complex economics of tourism and its hidden costs can undermine tourism's financial benefits for host countries. For example, income made from tourism may "leak" out of the local economy and be funneled to foreign-owned companies—only five percent of money spent by American tourists filters into the economies of developing host countries. Moreover, maintaining the costly infrastructure to support tourism can decrease government investment in important sectors such as education and health. Finally, countries that rely heavily on tourism for income are vulnerable to economic instability not only at home, but across the globe.

The tourism industry generates substantial economic benefits to both host countries and tourists' home countries. Especially in developing countries, one of the primary motivations for a region to promote itself as a tourism destination is the expected economic improvement.

As with other impacts, this massive economic development brings along both positive and negative consequences.

There are many hidden costs to tourism, which can have unfavorable economic effects on the host community. Often rich countries are better able to profit from tourism than poor ones. Whereas the least developed countries have the most urgent need for income, employment and general rise of the standard of living by means of tourism, they are least able to realize these benefits. Among the reasons for this are large-scale transfer of tourism revenues out of the host country and exclusion of local businesses and products.

Leakage

The direct income for an area is the amount of tourist expenditure that remains locally after taxes, profits, and wages are paid outside the area and after imports are purchased; these subtracted amounts are called leakage. In most all-inclusive package tours, about 80% of travelers' expenditures go to the airlines, hotels and other international companies (who often have their headquarters in the travelers' home countries), and not to local businesses or workers. In addition, significant amounts of income actually retained at destination level can leave again through leakage.

Local businesses often see their chances to earn income from tourists severely reduced by the creation of "all-inclusive" vacation packages.

Of each US$ 100 spent on a vacation tour by a tourist from a developed country, only around US$ 5 actually stays in a developing-country destination's economy. . . .

There are two main ways that leakage occurs:

Import leakage. This commonly occurs when tourists demand standards of equipment, food, and other products that the host country cannot supply. Especially in less-developed countries, food and drinks must often be imported, since local products are not up to the hotel's (i.e. tourist's) standards or the country simply doesn't have a supplying industry. Much of the income from tourism expenditures leaves the country again to pay for these imports.

The average import-related leakage for most developing countries today is between 40% and 50% of gross tourism earnings for small economies and between 10% and 20% for most advanced and diversified economies, according to UNCTAD.

Export leakage. Multinational corporations and large foreign businesses have a substantial share in the import leakage. Often, especially in poor developing destinations, they are the only ones that possess the necessary capital to invest in the construction of tourism infrastructure and facilities. As a consequence of this, an export leakage arises when overseas investors who finance the resorts and hotels take their profits back to their country of origin.

Enclave Tourism

Local businesses often see their chances to earn income from tourists severely reduced by the creation of "all-inclusive" vacation packages. When tourists remain for their entire stay at the same cruise ship or resort, which provides everything they need and where they will make all their expenditures, not much opportunity is left for local people to profit from tourism.

The Organization of American States (OAS) carried out a survey of Jamaica's tourist industry that looked at the role of the all-inclusives compared to other types of accommodation. It found that "All-inclusive hotels generate the largest amount of revenue but their impact on the economy is smaller per dollar of revenue than other accommodation subsectors."

It also concluded that all-inclusives imported more, and employed fewer people per dollar of revenue than other hotels. This information confirms the concern of those who have argued that all-inclusives have a smaller trickle-down effect on local economies.

The cruise ship industry provides another example of economic enclave tourism. . . . On many ships, especially in the Caribbean (the world's most popular cruise destination with 44.5% of cruise passengers), guests are encouraged to spend most of their time and money on board, and opportunities to spend in some ports are closely managed and restricted.

Other Negative Impacts

Infrastructure cost. Tourism development can cost the local government and local taxpayers a great deal of money. Developers may want the government to improve the airport, roads and other infrastructure, and possibly to provide tax breaks and other financial advantages, which are costly activities for the government. Public resources spent on subsidized infrastructure or tax breaks may reduce government investment in other critical areas such as education and health.

Increase in prices. Increasing demand for basic services and goods from tourists will often cause price hikes that negatively affect local residents whose income does not increase proportionately. A San Francisco State University study of Belize found that, as a consequence of tourism development, the prices for locals increased by 8%.

Tourism development and the related rise in real estate demand may dramatically increase building costs and land values. Not only does this make it more difficult for local people, especially in developing countries, to meet their basic daily needs, it can also result in a dominance by outsiders in land markets and in-migration that erodes economic opportunities for the locals, eventually disempowering residents. In Costa Rica, close to 65% of the hotels belong to foreigners. Long-term tourists, living in second homes, and the so-called amenity migrants (wealthy or retired people and liberal professionals moving to attractive destinations in order to enjoy the atmosphere and peaceful rhythms of life) cause price hikes in their new homes if their numbers attain a certain critical mass.

Economic dependence of the local community on tourism. Diversification in an economy is a sign of health; however, if a country or region becomes dependent for its economic survival upon one industry, it can put major stress upon this industry as well as the people involved to perform well. Many countries, especially developing countries with little ability to explore other resources, have embraced tourism as a way to boost the economy.

In The Gambia, for instance, 30% of the workforce depends directly or indirectly on tourism. In small island developing states, percentages can range from 83% in the Maldives to 21% in the Seychelles and 34% in Jamaica, according to the WTO. Over-reliance on tourism, especially mass tourism, carries significant risks to tourism-dependent economies. Economic recession and the impacts of natural disasters such as tropical storms and cyclones as well as changing tourism patterns can have a devastating effect on the local tourism sector.

Seasonal character of jobs. The seasonal character of the tourism industry creates economic problems for destinations that are heavily dependent on it. Problems that seasonal workers face include job (and therefore income) insecurity, usually with no guarantee of employment from one season to the next, difficulties in getting training, employment-related medical benefits, and recognition of their experience, and unsatisfactory housing and working conditions.

Other industry impacts affecting tourism. Economic crises, like the Asian crisis that hit Thailand, Malaysia and Indonesia, can be devastating to inbound tourism flows. The financial turmoil triggered a sharp fall in tourism flows to affected countries during 1997 and 1998. In the Philippines, the crisis and the temporary closure of Philippine Airlines affected inbound arrivals significantly as there was a decline of almost 3.3% in 1998.

5

Tourism Helps Preserve Indigenous Cultures

Alex Kerr

Alex Kerr is a writer based in Japan and Thailand. He is the author of several books on tourism in Japan.

Despite the bad reputation of tourists, tourism has helped to save many indigenous cultures that were threatened by encroaching modernization. In areas as diverse as Ecuador, Poland, and Japan, tourists have created demands for—and therefore resurgences in—traditional goods and services that were in danger of vanishing. Tourism has also contributed to the preservation of native architecture, housing, and communities. Most importantly, it encourages indigenous peoples' pride in their own culture and promotes meaningful cultural exchange. Indeed, tourism can be a vital force for the preservation of world cultures.

Nobody much likes tourists. They have a reputation for being loud, rude and disruptive. They are blamed for everything from prostitution to environmental degradation. "They want to have a good time, they are not well informed and want a short 'wow' factor," says Xavier Font, professor of tourism management at Britain's Leeds Metropolitan University. "Many locals see tourists as stupid."

Yet tourism may in fact be the true salvation of humankind's cultural heritage. After all, it's the main countervailing force to internationalization—that is, the global blah of TV, T shirts, tract housing, fast-food chains, business suits, malls and brand names. Internationalization has, in practice, been a process of everyone's coming to live and act the same; the Japanese gave up their kimonos because they were considered "unmodern," while Beijing destroyed its old city for the same reason. But tourists are looking for something old and something different—and they'll pay for it.

The souvenir trade . . . can almost singlehandedly keep fading cultures alive.

From the Brink of Extinction

The effect can be seen across the globe, rescuing traditional cities and cultures from the brink of extinction. Just five years ago [in 2003] the indigenous community of the Cayapas lived in little concrete houses with television sets, having moved from the banks of the Canande River in northwestern Ecuador to settle alongside the highway. They had nearly all abandoned the traditional hand-woven garb of their ancestors, and instead donned Nikes. "That's what progress meant to them," says Pedro Armend-Ariz, a tourism and development-planning engineer based in Quito. "It meant wearing tennis shoes and jeans, and having a TV so all the women could watch their soap operas every day."

Thanks to an influx of tourists, things have recently changed for the Cayapas. With visitors coming in search of community, or ethnic, tourism—to eat, work and often even live with the indigenous people—the Cayapas are embracing the nearly forgotten culture of their ancestors. Once again, they are wearing traditional clothes, building old-style homes and using traditional agricultural techniques. "They have become a sustainable community microbusiness, with a preservationist conscience, because they have understood that their indigenous roots are what interest tourists," says Armend-Ariz. "[It makes them] value their ancestral culture."

The situation is similar throughout Latin America, where interest in cultural and ecological tourism has been on the rise in recent years. Tourism to Guatemala, for example, with its Mayan heritage, lush rain forests and lakes surrounded by volcanoes, has doubled in the past decade to nearly 2 million foreign visitors a year. Their dollars have kept young indigenous women interested in learning the specialized craft of weaving on the Mayans' backstrap looms, says Alejandrina Silva, head of the Guatemalan Tourism Ministry's Cultural Heritage Office. "Indigenous artisanry forms an important part of the Guatemalan touristic product," she says. "If this were not the case, such crafts could die off and the younger generations would have to look for new trades that would allow them to survive."

Indeed, the souvenir trade—often maligned for promoting kitsch—can almost singlehandedly keep fading cultures alive. In the Tatra National Park in Zakopane, in southern Poland, the highlander tradition of making smoked sheep cheese—dying out among the younger generation—has earned a new lease on life thanks to tourists' desire for unforgettable souvenirs. Highlanders make the cheese, or *oscypek*, in their huts, forming it by hand and smoking it over a fire. Visitors feel free to chat with the locals as they watch, have a taste of the cheese and a glass of fresh goat's milk; most leave some money. They also snatch up the traditional clothing, wool hats, slippers and jackets—as well as sheep and goat cheese—on sale all over the city.

Whole cities owe their existence to tourism. After being designated World Heritage sites, Lijiang in southwestern China and Luang Prabang in Laos became meccas for tourists and, as a result, have managed to preserve their traditional feel. In Japan, tourism has sparked a new interest in Kyoto's old wooden *machiya* town houses, which were previously discarded as junk. Now real-estate agents specialize in finding and restoring *machiya*, and entrepreneurs fix them up as restaurants, boutiques or inns.

Of course the effects of tourism are not purely benign. Eventually tourism transforms old towns into something fundamentally different. Behind the façades of old houses in Lijiang, for example, you will find few original inhabitants today. They have been displaced by outside businessmen selling tourist trinkets. "The old places take on new clothes," Susan Fainstein, a professor at Columbia University and author of a book on tourism, *The City Builders*, has said. "The real places are scurrying to remake themselves to match the expectations of what people think they should be." Over time, tourism itself becomes a town's raison d'être. Nevertheless, a trinket-selling Lijiang is better than no Lijiang at all, and in the context of modern China's uncontrolled and breakneck development, the survival of a town like this verges on the miraculous.

A Healthy Competitive Edge

Tourism is not just about preserving old cultures; it can also influence modern ones. Catering to tourist whims provides a quick education for fledgling entrepreneurs, from the little boys in Angkor Wat pushing postcards, to the people who run small travel agencies, bed-and-breakfasts and coffee shops. Backpackers in particular, who have created their own cities-within-cities such as Khaosan Road in Bangkok, have sparked entrepreneurs to invent entirely new businesses, including herbal spas, meditation centers and home-stay programs.

For developed countries, tourism can help maintain a healthy competitive edge. Consider Japan, which until recently did not feel the need to court foreign travelers, and in the process nearly fell off the tourist map. The country ranks only 30th in the world as a tourist destination—about the same as Tunisia and Croatia. Without overseas visitors' clamoring for special services, hotels and inns rarely offer Internet access, ATM and mobile-phone networks won't link up with the rest of the world, and design and amenities at resorts lag behind world standards. Without tourists, modern culture fails to take the next step.

Of course, the biggest benefits of tourism may accrue to the tourists themselves. They go home having learned something about societies different from their own. And that, in the end, may do more good for the local cultures they visited than any amount of dollars. "When tourists from the Western world go to Third World countries, it increases the locals' pride in their own culture," says Ranjan Bandyopadhyay, a professor of tourism at Britain's Nottingham University. "Tourism is the avenue on which we can exchange our cultures and learn from each other. Tourism brings peace." Not to mention some really unforgettable smoked sheep-cheese souvenirs.

6

Tourism Threatens
Indigenous Cultures

Alison Johnston

Alison Johnston is director of the International Support Centre for Sustainable Tourism based in Vancouver, Canada.

The widely touted benefits of tourism for indigenous cultures mask the industry's deleterious impacts on world cultures. In truth, "politically correct" tourism, which is also known as "eco-tourism" or "sustainable" tourism, is a strategy of industrialized, historically colonial nations to access the vast natural resources indigenous people control and profit from their ways of life. These often government-backed programs force native and remote communities from their lands, essentially putting sacred sites, traditions, and heritages up for sale. Therefore, tourism, as a capitalist solution to social, economic, and environmental problems, must come to an end.

Today tourism is skidding on more than thin ice. Climate change is just one indictment this industry faces. Old questions about racism and colonialism also are simmering.

For the global consumer class, none of this is easy to decipher. One moment we listen to the BBC [British Broadcasting Corporation] or CNN [Cable News Network], and try to comprehend what it means that entire communities and peoples are being submerged by rising oceans. The next we are wooed as disaster tourists, told that we should float the polar bears,

Alison Johnston, "Tourism, Biodiversity and Indigenous Peoples: New Invitations for Social Change," *Third World Resurgence*, November/December, 2007. Reproduced by permission. www.twnside.org.sg/title2/resurgence/twr207-208.htm.

buoy the 'poor' and jumpstart nearly extinct cultures—all through tourism. In theory, our disposable income will fix what our throwaway society creates. How many of us really buy this?

In many cultural landscapes, tourism is a force for rapid culture loss.

Industry to industry, there is one model of doing business and it all centres on economic growth. Despite the replay of perilous impacts worldwide, we have been led to believe that tourism is somehow different. But industrial tourism is no gentler on the biosphere, or remote target communities, than extractive industries. In 2003 the UN [United Nations] Permanent Forum on Indigenous Issues reported that tourism causes severe damage to indigenous territories: the very places that world governments now profess to be safeguarding.

In many cultural landscapes, tourism is a force for rapid culture loss and, consequently, for immeasurable loss of biodiversity. Yet the success stories broadcasted tell us exactly the opposite. We hear about Aunt Maria selling her tamales and weavings, or of Elder Tom guiding international 'do-gooders' through his cultural odyssey of habitat conservation. Only inside affected communities are the real trade-offs of tourism normally voiced. Usually, these truths emerge slowly. It can be difficult for communities to retrace their decision making and admit that decisions were based on vulnerable hopes and/or partial facts. By the time real losses can be articulated, industry already has manipulated local poverty for privatised profits.

To understand these dynamics we need to look at 'eco' tourism. Through this lens we can begin to see the hidden cross-cultural dynamics of global trade. We get a glimpse of where exactly corporations are racing (besides the oilfields) and why indigenous peoples, in particular, are vigilant.

Rethinking Indigenous Peoples' Experiences

Since ecotourism emerged in the mid-1980s as the 'development' miracle, it has been in steady disrepute at the community level. Two decades into this controversy, industry is still giving it a makeover. Today, the favourite terminology is 'sustainable' tourism. Governments portray tourism as the answer to both poverty and environmental conservation—with an emphasis on protecting biodiversity. Who could object?

This conservation agenda is not finding acceptance among indigenous peoples, the poorest of the poor globally due to colonialism. Worldwide, indigenous ancestral territories hold the bulk of the world's remaining resources. When 'biodiversity' programming aimed at these areas interferes with customary law—allowing industrial access and use, and ultimately degradation (culturally, viewed as desecration)—there usually is conflict.

'Eco' tourism, and the 'protected' areas advanced with it, are concepts that originated with Northern conservation groups. Both concepts differ significantly from indigenous peoples' own principles for conservation. There have been attempts to validate each by comparing them with common customary practices, such as hosting and guardianship. However, ancestral title is fundamentally distinct from conservation for industrial purposes. It links rights to responsibilities—addressing all levels of responsibility (including the spiritual) as an indivisible (that is, sacred) whole, incumbent on one and all from birth.

This has led indigenous leaders to be increasingly careful about how they incorporate any 'biodiversity' initiative into new relationships with government, industry, development agencies or NGOs. Already, most protected areas tourism either involves or impacts indigenous peoples. 'There are currently some 60,000 protected areas in the world, the majority of which have been established on Indigenous Peoples' lands without their consent'. As a result, indigenous lands now rank among the world's most profitable 'eco' tourism destinations. Yet indigenous peoples themselves are increasingly impoverished.

Globally, targeted indigenous peoples . . . are rarely informed of, or meaningfully consulted on, national tourism strategies.

Most indigenous peoples are finding that industrial 'eco' tourism undermines their very basis for survival. It is a tool for governments to alienate their ancestral lands for commerce. Once forced off their lands, they cannot so easily assert their rights based on continuous occupancy and use. Nor can they feed themselves without taking a job. Thus, poverty is actually induced and cultural practices are methodically interrupted. Then, in a perverse twist, the 'eco' tourism industry markets endangered cultures (the 'exotic')—as if commercialisation of a people does no harm. Brochures splash stolen cultural images worldwide.

These economic trends are a profound concern to indigenous leaders continent to continent. Globally, targeted indigenous peoples—such as the Karen of Thailand, Maasai of Kenya and Tanzania, and Maya of Central America—are rarely informed of, or meaningfully consulted on, national tourism strategies. Their right to prior informed consent is routinely ignored. The industry standard is exploitation, despite protections existing in international law.

The full extent of this cycle of abuse, for humanity, is poorly understood. At first glance it appears that the issues are isolated. But when we look closer it is clear that no one is immune from the impacts.

Today, the 'eco' tourism industry is fronting one of the most dangerous enterprises in our global economy. It is selling indigenous peoples' sacred sites, ceremonies and ancestral knowledge. We can see this at Uluru in Australia, Machu Picchu in Peru and the Drakensburg area of South Africa, among countless other places. What is the significance? This casual appropriation of 'private' aspects of culture undermines customary governance systems at their core. It tampers with something few of us comprehend.

Through tourism, our governments are actively colonising, while seeming to praise cultural diversity and its vital link to biodiversity conservation. They are suppressing the very cultural value systems which underlie 'biodiversity' (really, life systems on Earth). So far, most of us passively stand by.

Watching the Colonial Tactics of the North

In the same years that ecotourism grew, the topic of 'neo-colonialism' resurfaced due to ongoing violations of indigenous rights economy-wide, especially the right to self-determination. The World Council of Indigenous Peoples (WCIP) had formed in 1975, linking peoples through their common histories. By the 1980s indigenous peoples were actively comparing notes on present-day colonial tactics. At that time, indigenous peoples across the North were reeling from a new wave of assimilation policies. Those in the South, meanwhile, were either bracing against the 'green gold' rush, or fending off poverty-hungry venture capitalists. Continent to continent, it was clear that the racist *terra nullius* [nobody's land] concept (casting indigenous ancestral lands as vacant and 'up for grabs') still dictated commerce. So the WCIP coordinated efforts to plant indigenous rights on the UN agenda, utilising nation states' own language of international law.

For colonial allies such as Canada, Australia, New Zealand, the United States and Great Britain, the prospect of tribal unity across continents was startling. Like other industrial nation states, they were accustomed to manoeuvring without much scrutiny. Now there was new tension to dialogues on trade and 'aid'. The Russell Tribunals in Europe had put a spotlight on the systemic annihilation and exploitation of indigenous peoples. Simultaneously, the anti-apartheid movement had grown, and lobby groups noticed these industrialists' own avoidance of reconciliation. Countries that previously felt immune to issues raised by the UN Committee on Decolonisation were suddenly in a pinch.

Even before the Brundtland Report famously linked equity with 'sustainable development', this core group of industrial nations was searching for a charismatic makeover. By the late 1980s, rhetoric on stakeholder consultation and community participation was buzzing in 'development' circles. In 'eco' tourism, colonial governments of the North had found a reliable decoy. They pushed it as much at home as abroad.

Now, in all directions, the colonial pattern repeats itself. Since 2004 Australia has associated its national tourism brand with spirituality, capitalising on Uluru, sacred site of the Anangu. While profiting off indigenous cultures, it has legislated oppressive controls in Aboriginal communities. Next door in New Zealand similar forces are at play. This year [in 2007] New Zealand released its Tourism Strategy 2015, announcing that the Maori principle of *kaitiakitanga* (guardianship) would guide conservation measures. Within days several Maori activists were arrested as terrorists. Similarly, Canada's recent spending spree on Aboriginal cultural centres—for tourism—has coincided with its continuing efforts to extinguish Aboriginal title and rights. All the while, these nations move in unison to water down indigenous rights at the UN.

The goal of today's Northern colonial powers is to pursue what is left of world 'resources' in a more politically correct way. The UN Convention on Biological Diversity (CBD) was elaborated, alongside companion trade agreements, to ease the way. Its text recognises the link between cultural and biological diversity but was purposely saddled with contradictions. All provisions for safeguarding traditional knowledge are offset by colonial caveats. The economic integration of indigenous peoples has been expedited, with tourism designated an official avenue.

Choosing Social Change

Under the CBD, the main thrust is financial incentives for conservation—utilising conventional economic models. The UN guidelines on tourism and biodiversity never did pass through any process with indigenous peoples. This was avoided, since the guidelines would not withstand scrutiny against rights.

Tourism needs to be cleansed of the ugly 'isms', before we can talk of any positive 'eco' effect.

There is now a steady flow of policy initiatives advancing mass 'eco' tourism: from the CBD Secretariat's current workshops pushing indigenous tourism (launched in the Canadian Arctic, as if the Inuit are happy to politically endorse their own sinking) to the forthcoming UNESCO/IUCN [United Nations Educational, Scientific, and Cultural Organization/ International Union for Conservation of Nature] guidelines on managing sacred natural sites within 'protected' areas (suggesting prior informed consent where none exists). What these initiatives do is isolate dialogue within a single political realm: the colonial governance system. Business ambassadors are sought out, while customary authorities and rights advocates are sidelined.

Climate change is symptomatic of this governance chaos. The danger now is that the issue of climate change may be manipulated into another decoy, to avoid redressing deeper issues such as colonialism. If we choose to ignore this, and disregard cultural protocols for keeping balance (including their spiritual dimensions), we invite global meltdown. We create a situation where whole generations—regardless of race, class and geography—will experience environmental havoc and trauma.

The gift in our lap right now is the UN Declaration on the Rights of Indigenous Peoples, passed in September 2007. This document is the legacy of the World Council of Indigenous Peoples. Its content draws on existing international law concerning the rights of peoples, and therefore says nothing new or revolutionary. However, this redundancy is its value. The declaration reminds us that we already have the knowledge and tools necessary for new relationships.

Let's not make the UN Declaration on the Rights of Indigenous Peoples another false idol, like the CBD or 'eco' tourism, distracting us from the underlying issues and real work. Colonialism has divided us but the earth is demanding our reconnection. It is time to value introspection, cultivate gentleness (that is, respect) and heal the intergenerational dysfunction long marketed as progress. There will be no 'eco' solutions without getting to know ourselves and each other, outside colonial typecasting and beyond the 'consumer' labels thrust on us all by industry.

Tourism needs to be cleansed of the ugly 'isms', before we can talk of any positive 'eco' effect.

7

Tourism Contributes to the Exploitation of Women and Children

Janice Shaw Crouse, Ph.D. and Anne Stover

Janice Shaw Crouse, Ph.D., BLI's Senior Fellow, is a member of the Washington, D.C.-based Initiative Against Sexual Trafficking, the World Evangelical Fellowship's Task Force Against Abuse of Women and Children and Concerned Women for America's policy director for sexual trafficking issues. Anne Stover, a senior at Asbury College, is a summer intern at the Beverly LaHaye Institute.

The following viewpoint argues that global tourism perpetuates the sexual and economic exploitation of women as well as their social oppression. Although attempts have been made to prosecute tourists for sex crimes against minors, not much progress has been made. The Australian government is trying to legalize prostitution because of the high numbers of tourists who come for their sex industry, but this will not help anyone. It is important that people become more aware of sex tourism and the global effects it has on women and children.

Sex Trafficking is a worldwide problem with ties to the underbelly of multi-national big businesses and to international thugs and gangsters of the worst kinds. The United States State Department estimates that over 2 million women and children are abducted and forced into sexual slavery every

Janice Shaw Crouse, Anne Stover, "Sex Tourism Binds Nations In An Appalling Alliance," Concerned Women for America, July 18, 2002.

year. One wrinkle on this tragic problem is the growing sex-tourism industry—a despicable development that is binding nations in appalling alliances. What is happening in Australia and Cambodia reflects the worldwide linkages of sex trafficking, sexual slavery and sex tourism.

Legalizing Prostitution Helps No One

The Australian government is currently trying to tidy-up their sex tourism problem by keeping the sex tourists home; they are trying to pass legislation that would decriminalize and legalize street prostitution. Government officials have suggested "tolerance zones" for prostitutes to legally solicit, and "safe houses" where prostitutes could service their clients out of sight. Among those leading the charge is a woman who suggested tolerance zones nearly 20 years ago, Professor Marcia Neave, who is now the state's Law Reform Commissioner. She also helped create Victoria's first legal brothels. These efforts have not discouraged street prostitution, nor has legalizing prostitution healed the social problems created by illegal prostitution. The drug trade has not slowed and the number of street sex workers in areas where prostitution is legal continues to grow.

Child welfare workers in Cambodia estimate that every year several hundred Australian sex tourists take advantage of Cambodia's convenient geographic proximity to feed their pedophilic desires.

Residents of St. Kilda, Australia, have described their town as an "open-air brothel." According to The Melbourne Age, "Residents are confronted with sex acts in lanes, in their front gardens, and in cars outside their homes." In addition, residents feel threatened by the pimps and spotters who lurk in the shadows. Sexually transmitted diseases have also increased. According to the Sydney Sexual Health Center, it is estimated that up to 50 percent of adults have an STD, and of the 10 million Australians in the sexually active age group: 1 in 3 has a strain of genital warts and at least 1 in 5 has genital herpes. The only thing tolerance zones and safe houses have secured is an environment for sexually transmitted diseases and the continuation of sexual, physical and emotional abuse.

At the same time, Australia is turning a blind eye on legislation it passed to end sex crimes against minors in Cambodia by Australian sex tourists. What Australian sex shoppers cannot satisfy legally in Australia, they are satisfying without fear of prosecution in Cambodia. Child welfare workers in Cambodia estimate that every year several hundred Australian sex tourists take advantage of Cambodia's convenient geographic proximity to feed their pedophilic desires.

Protecting Minors

In 1994, legislation was introduced to prosecute Australian tourists for sex crimes against minors. However, Australian authorities have not attempted to prosecute cases against Australian sex tourists in Cambodia since 1996 when an attempt to prosecute former Australian diplomat to Phnom Penh, John Holloway, failed. Australian authorities continue to alert Cambodian authorities of suspected pedophiles, but no one is prosecuting.

It is estimated that there are 20,000 children involved in the child sex industry in Cambodia. In Svay Pak, an impoverished town near Phnom Penh, the number of brothels has doubled in five years selling children as young as 9 years old for sex to Australian sex tourists, according to the *Melbourne Age*. Yet both Australian and Cambodian authorities are abandoning their campaigns designed to stop Australian pedophiles from harming Cambodia's children. Part of the problem, according to Australian ambassador to Cambodia Louise Hand, is getting the local authorities to act on the information the Australian Embassy gives them. Local officials are making more money protecting sex tourists than by protecting their weakest citizens.

Bernadette McMenamin, head of the Australian branch of ECPAT (End Child Prostitution, Pornography and Trafficking), said, "there is something terribly wrong in Cambodia." But she is forgetting that there is also something terribly wrong in Australia. Even worse, and tragically, what is happening in both countries simply reflects the sex trafficking and sexual slavery that is happening—and being ignored—all around the world.

8

Tourists Should Not Be Deterred by Terrorism

Tony Abbott

Tony Abbott is a member of the Cabinet of Australia. He was assigned to the Shadow Ministry of Families, Community Services and Indigenous Affairs in December 2007.

In recent years, terrorist attacks and activity in destinations such as Indonesia's Bali and Egypt have set the tourism industry into decline. Terrorists have targeted these popular holiday destinations because they are in nonconformist Muslim countries and because they wish to cause economic damage and terrorize foreigners and infidels. However, the developing economies of Indonesia (which was battered by the Asian tsunami of 2004), Egypt, and other countries depend heavily on tourism, and tourists should not let terrorist organizations deter them from keeping tourism thriving and supporting pluralism in Muslim countries.

So far, no country has escaped from Third World status on the basis of foreign aid. Every country that has moved out of comparative poverty (such as Korea, Taiwan and Singapore) and every region that has become a particular country's economic locomotive (such as Mumbai or Shanghai) has done so on the basis of trade, not aid.

This stands to reason because buying from someone makes him a partner while giving to someone is more likely to make

Tony Abbott, "The Moral Imperative For Tourists," *Sydney Morning Herald*, July 19, 2006. Copyright © 2006. The Sydney Morning Herald. Reproduced by permission. www.smh.com.au/news/opinion/the-moral-imperative-for tourists/2006/7/18/1153166377695.html?page=fullpage#contentSwap1.

him a supplicant than a friend. Aid is important, especially in times of trouble such as after the Asian tsunami of 2004, but not nearly as important as a market economy to the foundation of lasting wealth and self-respect.

This reflection was prompted by a recent trip to Bali, which tourism has lifted from being one of the poorest parts of Indonesia to being one of the most prosperous parts. It was gratifying to think that indulging in a five-star lifestyle at a fraction of what it would cost in Australia and enjoying some remarkably good value shopping might be helping to reduce world poverty and equalise the gap between rich and poor. Tourists have never been accorded much moral standing but it seems they are just as necessary as aid workers and might be of more long-term benefit for the world's poorest countries.

A recent report by the Australian Co-operative Research Centre for Sustainable Tourism noted that tourism accounts for 36 per cent of trade in commercial services in advanced economies but 66 per cent of such trade in developing countries. Tourism is the only service industry where the Third World as a whole has a positive balance of trade with the First World: a $6 billion surplus in 1980 rising to nearly $9 billion in 1998. In addition, international tourism in developing countries is increasing by 9.5 per cent a year compared to 4.6 per cent worldwide.

Unsurprisingly, the report warns that tourism is too important to be left to the private sector and worries about the effect of foreign tourism on local culture. Still, it concedes that all forms of modernisation change indigenous cultures and notes tourism is a growing and significant part of the economy in all but one of the 12 countries that are home to 80 per cent of the world's poor. Tourism, it concludes, "appears to be one of the few economic sectors able to guide a number of developing countries to higher levels of prosperity and for some to leave behind their least-developed country status".

A Patriotic Thing to Do

If economic deprivation breeds resentment, and tourism is an important means to economic development, it's no wonder terrorist groups have targeted tourism in countries such as Egypt and Indonesia. Targeting places such as Bali's Sari night-club not only punishes the decadent infidel but helps to wreck the local economy in places which fail to conform to any zealot's blueprint. Last year's bombings in Bali, targeting families in cafes, were presumably designed to demonstrate that no one is safe and were a form of economic warfare against the people there.

Taking a holiday in Indonesia is riskier than going to the Gold Coast, but may ultimately be quite a patriotic thing to do.

The Federal Government rightly warns people about the dangers of travel in countries such as Indonesia, and people should be sensible about the potential risks involved. In 2003, in the aftermath of the 2002 bombing at Kuta, tourist arrivals in Bali were almost 40 per cent down on 2001. Even so, by 2004 tourist numbers had exceeded the previous peak. Australian tourists had increased by 10 per cent on the previous record. There are no official figures yet for this year but one hotel says September bookings are back to last year's level.

In any event, Australians' nervousness about security is in contrast to fondness for something different and enthusiasm for a good deal.

People who have no desire to court trouble or to make political statements can be conscious of the importance of Indonesia to Australia and reluctant to have their choices dictated to them. The most culturally oblivious tourist is still adding to our collective awareness of our vast neighbour as well as building the Indonesian economy, which is only a quarter the size of Australia's with 10 times the population.

Then there's the importance of preserving a Muslim country which is relatively easygoing, culturally pluralist and democratic. Taking a holiday in Indonesia is riskier than going to the Gold Coast, but may ultimately be quite a patriotic thing to do.

9

Tourism Will Be Affected by Climate Change

Elisabeth Rosenthal

Elisabeth Rosenthal is an award-winning journalist and a trained physician. She is the health, science, and environment correspondent for the International Herald Tribune.

Tourist activity is closely linked to the world's climate, and the current trend of global warming is increasing its impact on the industry. Travel associated with tourism accounts for approximately five percent of global carbon dioxide emissions, and reducing air travel and going "green" could cripple the tourism industries in developing countries. Moreover, climbing temperatures pose a threat to pristine beaches, biologically diverse coral reefs, glaciers, and snowfall patterns, which can eliminate the seasonal recreations of tourists. A few destinations, however, are benefiting from global warming—golfing season in Antalya, Turkey, has been extended by over a month because of warmer weather.

It is often said that farmers are on the front lines dealing with global warming, their livelihoods being extraordinarily dependent on the weather. But tour operators and resort owners are not far behind.

Imagine a ski resort whose chairlifts are in the lower reaches of mountains, without decent snow. Or a scuba club whose reefs succumbed to warmer and stormier seas. Or a golfing hotel in a district where water shortages made it im-

Elisabeth Rosenthal, "Changing Climate Haunts Tourism," *International Herald Tribune*, October 30, 2007, www.iht.com/articles/2007/10/30/business/tourism.php?WT.mc_id=rssfrontpage.

possible to keep fairways green. All are real possibilities, industry experts say, and in fact, early effects are already being felt.

And so, this month [October 2007], the United Nations convened a conference, "Climate Change and Tourism," for tour operators and officials from nearly 100 countries to discuss the impact of global warming on their livelihoods. "The tourism industry must adapt rapidly," the final report concluded.

The entire tourism product will be affected—every destination has a climate-related component.

"The entire tourism product will be affected—every destination has a climate-related component," Geoffrey Lipman, assistant secretary general of the UN [United Nations] World Tourism Organization, said by telephone from the meeting, held in Davos, Switzerland. If the climate is going to change, "which we know it will, we'd all better adapt," he said.

"Some people are going to find that they had tourism before and don't now," Lipman said. "In the Canadian Rockies it may be the reverse."

In the developed world, tour operators do not generally face a crisis, though profits will depend on successful adjustment. But along the equator, keeping the tourist industry afloat is often a matter of national survival. In much of Africa for instance, tourism is the major source of income and often the only source of foreign currency.

Yet there is a heavy cost. With the industry's reliance on cars and buses, air-conditioning and especially air travel, tourism is a major source of warming gasses. It accounts for about 5 percent of the world's carbon dioxide emissions, the Davos conference concluded. And poor countries normally do not have the money to make any eco-friendly changes.

"It's nice to talk about reducing air travel but many nation states depend on it," said Lipman, of the UN tourism organization. "Think about what happens to New Zealand and Australia. More important, what happens to poor countries—the Maldives, Seychelles and Africa—who need it because it is the only way to get tourists in."

Intimately Intertwined

Recognizing that tourism and climate change are intimately intertwined, Fiji combined its Ministries of the Environment and Tourism this summer.

"Tourism is *the* vehicle for poverty alleviation in Fiji— that's how important it has become," said Banuve Kaumaito-toya, permanent secretary of Fiji's new Ministry of Tourism and Environment, who attended the Davos conference. "Without it, our economy would collapse. So we have to plan to mitigate and adapt to climate change."

For some destinations, both warm and cold, climate change is already having an impact on tourism and planning.

In Fiji more frequent storms that scientists say are caused by warming are eroding mountains and driving dirt and fresh water into the sea. That threatens to erode pristine beaches, and endangers coral reefs which need considerable salt in the water.

Fijian planners are trying to gauge the course of such change and set new standards, like guidelines for how far above the water bungalows should be built to be safe if the sea level rises. "At the moment the effect is subtle, but we don't want our reefs—our island—to disappear," Kaumaito-toya said.

At the Whistler Blackcomb Ski Resort in Canada, glaciers are receding and good snow is found higher up the mountain than 10 years ago. "We've been building lifts higher, in more snow-reliant zones to give us more stability," said Arthur De Jong, the mountain planning and environment resource manager at the resort.

Ski lifts last 25 years, De Jong said. To decide where to place new ones, the resort has run a mix of computer simulations to try to determine where the snow will be depending on varying calculations of how much the temperature might rise over 30 years.

In addition, the resort has a broader green plan. It is making energy to run the lifts from snow runoff on the mountain. Its ski village is car free. And the resort has diversified from snow and it now has a booming summer business as well.

Going Green Is Expensive

But undertaking new engineering projects and computer simulations take money and expertise that are in short supply in much of the world.

"Adaptation is expensive and the finances are a big challenge for [a] place like Kenya," said Judith Gona, executive director of Ecotourism Kenya, which is trying to make that country's travel industry greener.

"In recent years Kenya has become a mass tourism destination—hotels were built to hold as many people as possible. Things like air-conditioning systems are not very efficient."

"It is difficult to put money into green, even if people know they should."

In the short term, global warming provides opportunities too, especially in temperate zones. Warming trends have lengthened the golfing season in Antalya, Turkey, by over a month, said Ugur Budak, golf coordinator of Akkanat Holdings there.

Golfing used to begin in March. But tourists from Britain and Germany are now coming to Antalya in February. "Winters are milder so the effect on us for now is good," Budak said. So far there had not been problems like the water shortages experienced in other parts of the world, he said, "But we know we could be vulnerable in the future."

At the end of the Davos conference, the UN World Tourism Organization advised travelers to take the climate into account and "where possible to reduce their carbon footprint." But if Europeans stop flying to Fiji or Antalya, poverty will worsen, tourism officials said.

10

Tourism Threatens World Landmarks

Mac Margolis

Mac Margolis is a freelance writer and a correspondent for Newsweek International.

Tourism is taking a heavy toll on world landmarks and natural wonders. Popular historic tourist attractions such as Machu Picchu, the Great Wall of China, and Luxor are crumbling due to the pounding traffic of tourists. In addition, entire culturally rich cities such as Mexico City, Venice, and New Orleans are edging close to, or have almost succumbed to, environmental disaster. Even remote destinations, such as Antartica, are not safe from tourism's reach. However, tourism can be transformed into a force that fortifies conservation and preserves world heritages, and meeting this challenge is in the hands of today's generation.

When Ernest Hemingway wrote *The Snows of Kilimanjaro*, a holiday outing was the last thing he had in mind. Who could have known that this classic tale about a failed writer dying of gangrene in the shadow of Africa's tallest mountain would spark a stampede? Every year, some 10,000 vacationers huff their way to the 5,896-meter peak that untold tour operators have flogged with Hemingway's majestic words: "Wide as all the world, great, high, and unbelievably white in the sun." So it's poetic justice of sorts that the travel industry's purloined icon is melting. Thanks to global warming and deforestation, the millennial snowcap that was said to cover King Solomon's tomb is receding. Scientists say that within 15 years, Kilimanjaro's storied glaciers will be history. Soon the brokers of wanderlust may be spinning the prose again to hawk the ultimate vacation: "Last chance to see the snows of Kilimanjaro."

The number-one threat to tourist treasures, paradoxically, is tourism itself.

Those vanishing snows are emblematic of travel in a worrying new time—when no place can be taken for granted anymore. No matter how exotic the destination, until recently a traveler's biggest concern was how to get there, not where the journey would ultimately lead. Now thanks to rising incomes and falling airfares, getting there is the easy part; last year a record 806 million tourists hit the road. But those hordes— combined with forces ranging from climate change to civil war, industrial toxins to runaway development—are laying siege to some of the world's most treasured and irreplaceable sites. Whether the millennial gates of Machu Picchu or the moonlit waterways of Venice, we are in danger of losing places we thought would always be around, sure as Stonehenge. . . . New Orleans nearly drowned. The Coral Triangle, a diver's paradise, is as fragile as an eggshell. Visitors ride go-karts along the Great Wall of China and steal artifacts from the crumbling temples of Luxor. Even Stonehenge has been cordoned off. The only certainty for today's travelers is that the wonders of the world are perishable, whether they're made of stone or ice, by man or nature.

"Unsustainable Tourism"

The number-one threat to tourist treasures, paradoxically, is tourism itself. The challenge is how to keep the world's most esteemed monuments from being loved to death. "Tourism carries a tremendous potential that must be acknowledged as essential for the future of world heritage," says Bonnie Burnham, president of the World Monuments Fund (WMF). "But without proper management we can easily get out of control." For all Hurricane Wilma's wrath, patching Cancun back together will be easy compared with taming the monster that the tourist economy has unleashed. The 7 million visitors a year who descend on this megaresort and surrounding patches of the Mexican Caribbean coast already represent a conservation nightmare, straining water supply, sewers, and marine life. And it's not just Mexico. Conservation International reckons that "unsustainable tourism" poses the main threat to half the cultural heritage sites in Latin America and the Caribbean, and to one in five sites in Asia and the Pacific. Cambodia's once-remote Angkor temples now receive a million visitors a year; the Taj Mahal is subject to 7 million. Rising prosperity in the developing world, more and more elderly on the move, and cheap flights to anywhere will only hasten the human flood. China alone reported a staggering 1.1 billion domestic tourists in 2004.

Our wanderlust is not solely to blame, however. Popular tourist destinations have been hit in the last few years by glacier-withering global warming, an epic tidal wave and a harem of tropical storms in the Caribbean. Worse, avian flu is on the loose. Before leaving home the future holidaymaker may be obliged to consult not only the exchange rate and the Weather Channel but the Tsunami Warning Center, Jane's Terrorism Watch Report ("your daily update on terrorist activities worldwide") and Citigroup's Pandemic Sensitivity Index. The hazards have not been lost on the travel industry, the world's largest earner of foreign exchange. For the first time, the World Trade and Tourism Council (WTTC) will dedicate an entire session of its annual summit, to be held in Washington next month [May 2006], to health and natural disasters. "Whether it's natural or manmade catastrophes, this is the reality," says WTTC chairman Vince Wolfington. "And more and more we're going to have to deal with it."

A Daunting Task

It is a daunting task. The WMF list of the 100 most endangered world heritage sites spans 55 countries. Topping the list: Iraq—not the Iraq Museum or the Al Askariya shrine, but the entire country. Never mind the obvious threats, like terrorism, war or sectarian strife. Forces like global warming pose subtler challenges. The United Nations University recently reported that the number of annual catastrophes provoked by "extreme weather" and water-related emergencies has tripled since the 1970s, while economic damage increased sixfold. By now everyone knows that Venice is drowning, but even such apparently untouchable monuments as the Tower of London and the adobe mosques of Timbuktu are also vulnerable, thanks to the flash floods and rising water tables caused by global climate change. While Bourbon Street was tidied up in time for Mardi Gras, so much of the rest of New Orleans remains in shambles that hotels have been forced to cede rooms to homeless employees. The whole city has been added to the WMF's most endangered list.

The threats have literally reached the ends of the earth. Most holidaymakers shiver at the thought of a trek to Antarctica. Not Tom Ritchie. "To be in a small boat and see a huge humpback whale come up and look at you is a spiritual interaction," says Ritchie, a guide for Lindblad Expeditions. Today travelers shell out up to $50,000 for a romp on the White Continent—a small price to pay for an opportunity that may not be around in 30 years. Scientists report that 212 of the 244 glaciers necklacing the Antarctic Peninsula have retreated as temperatures have risen more than 4.5 degrees Fahrenheit in the past 60 years. Whales and penguins that feed on krill and coldwater plankton may soon be gone—along with one of the world's most cherished photo ops.

Predatory economic development has done its share of damage as well. The tower at the Helsinki Malmi international airport is a gem of 1930s modernist architecture, but if city developers have their way, it will be razed to make way for a 10,000-unit suburban housing complex. If saving a building sounds daunting, think about rescuing an entire city. If Mexico City (population: 18 million) keeps on sucking up ground water at the current clip from the city's aquifer, the world's largest megalopolis—which also happens to contain the world's finest pre-Columbian ruins—is certain to sink into the clay. No wonder all of Mexico City, too, has been relegated to the WMF's endangered list. Nor is the Old World safe from the ravages of the modern. Though seismologists say that Vesuvius will erupt again sooner or later, hot lava may be the least of the worries facing Naples, a city of 1 million nestled in the volcano's shadow. In its glory, in the 17th century, Naples was Europe's largest city after Paris and every bit as cosmopolitan. These days, Naples might look more like a postcard for urban decadence. Chaotic traffic has pumped so much poison into the air that the façades of medieval buildings are disintegrating. Urban hucksters hurl up four clandestine buildings for every legal one, turning this U.N. World Heritage site into a boneyard of scaffolding. "See Naples and Die," the Bourbons once boasted during Naples's golden age. Skeptics have a new saying: "See Naples before it dies."

The good—and bad—news is that tourists come from hardy stock. Just a year after the Asian tsunami swallowed hundreds of kilometers of South Asian beachfront, vacationers came streaming back. Sometimes calamity can be turned into opportunity. "There definitely is a rush to see and explore the world before it changes," says Matt Kareus of Natural Habitat, which operates excursions to Antarctica. Archeologists and green groups blame the massive Three Gorges hydroelectric dam for destroying untold centuries-old cultural splendors, but Chinese sightseers line up to snap pictures from the concrete ramparts. Even the empty space where the World Trade towers once stood has become a tourist attraction. "We are all aware the world is more unpredictable," says Julio Aramberri, professor of tourism at Philadelphia's Drexel University. "But tourism is much more resilient than you'd think."

Managing the Onslaught

Managing the onslaught is now a topic of fierce debate. "Sometimes it takes coming to the brink of loss to make people recognize what they value," says Burnham. Listing endangered sites helps raise their visibility and rally local support, but can also backfire by unleashing more tourists for a final antediluvian glimpse. Steeper admission prices help, but are blatantly biased toward travelers with deeper pockets. Some experts are turning to crowd engineering, such as timed tickets, a technique that many museums and Disney World mastered years ago. UNESCO's [United Nations Educational, Scientific, and Cultural Organization] World Heritage Centre channels money to safeguard sites, while the WMF works with local governments, civic groups and the private sector to restore imperiled monuments.

The debate is hardly academic. By now it's apparent that travelers may be spooked, delayed or detoured, but not deterred. Despite the chain of calamities, more people than ever left home on holiday last year, and experts are confident the numbers will continue to grow. A world awash in tourists can be a curse for its endangered treasures, or a source of funds to save them. Getting the balance right could be the difference between future generations beholding the living wonders of the world, and merely reading about them in a story book.

11

Ecotourism Helps Protect the Environment

Eviana Hartman with Christina Cavaliere

Eviana Hartman is the Eco Wise columnist for the Washington Post. *Christina Cavaliere is the director of training and education for the International Ecotourism Society.*

Ecotourism is ecologically responsible travel to natural environments that conserves local communities and cultures. The authenticity of ecotourism programs and packages can be assessed by determining several factors: the ecological impacts and energy efficiency of facilities and services such as hotels and transportation, whether local people are employed at different levels, how the travel experience ties in with the natural environment and regional culture, and if the host community directly benefits from the profits. Travel, in reality, takes place every day, and every individual can take simple measures to do it sustainably.

Some of you have written to ask: Is sustainable travel, also known as eco-tourism, a contradiction in terms? Christina Cavaliere doesn't think so. The Dupont Circle resident, 30, has studied tribal forestry in Ecuador, taught English in Thailand, worked on a farm in Costa Rica and earned a master's degree in tourism and sustainable development in Australia—not to mention her time spent traveling in Cambodia, Ghana, India, France and other countries.

Now, as director of training and education for the International Ecotourism Society [TIES]—a D.C.-based organization

Eviana Hartman with Christina Cavaliere, "See the Planet, Save the Planet," *Washington Post*, February 10, 2008. Reproduced by permission of the authors. http://www.washingtonpost.com/wp-dyn/content/article/2008/02/07/AR2008020703740.html.

devoted to promoting sustainable travel—she hopscotches around the globe working to make the industry greener. We talked with Cavaliere to find out how to travel light—on the planet, that is.

Defining Eco-tourism

How do you define eco-tourism?

Eco-tourism is responsible travel to natural areas or nature-based areas that conserves the environment and improves the well-being of local people.

As with all things "green," eco-tourism experiences aren't always as planet-sensitive as they make themselves out to be. How can someone tell the difference?

There are certain things you can look at:

- Is a hotel minimizing impact in any way that they can: green building, conservation of resources such as water? Look at the built environment and cultural awareness and respect.

- See if the local community is employed at multiple levels: not just housekeepers and cooks, but management positions.

- Is the built environment marrying and matching with the natural environment, or is it obviously not a sustainably built dwelling?

- Does it provide a positive experience? Is there a direct cultural or environmental interpretation or educational experience? That's an important part of being sustainable.

- Does it provide direct financial empowerment of the local community? It should be easy to find out or see. How sensitive is it to the host country's political, environmental and social climate?

Some argue that no travel to delicate and endangered ecosystems can really be called sustainable.

I certainly think that there's a need for the tourism industry and for individual consumers to change travel patterns and travel behavior. . . . But I am a huge advocate, because I've seen that sustainable travel is a successful form of environmental and social conservation. It brings business opportunities that allow money and information generation to happen inside a community. When that economic opportunity is not there, traditional extractions of natural resources continue to occur.

Sustainable travel is a successful form of environmental and social conservation.

What about the climate change question? Flying certainly produces a lot of carbon dioxide.

One of the worst environmental actions you can do is to buy a plane ticket. I started, with some other partners, an advocacy camp called Traveling With Climate in Mind. We started communicating to individual tourists and businesses about what they can do. Individually, there are many ways you can mitigate carbon emissions. Instead of traveling six times a year for three days, travel once a year for three weeks. When you get to the destination, choose carbon-neutral activities. Rent a bike. Walk to your destinations. Go on nature walks instead of renting jet skis or anything that uses petrol.

Do you buy carbon offsets to account for the emissions from your travel?

Yes, all of our staff here at TIES does. I travel quite a bit with this position. Last year we held an international conference that had 76 countries and 470 people, and we offset the entire event and everyone's flights.

What about the perception that eco-tourism is expensive? What can people on a tight budget do?

In the nonprofit world, we have a joke that the hours are long but at least the pay isn't very good. I've done all my travel on a shoestring budget. . . . You spend less when you're buying from local businesses and staying in local accommodations, and you're not locked away in the compound of a major international resort. Also, you certainly don't need to travel internationally to have a sustainable travel experience. . . . Rock Creek Park is a wonderful example of a nature-based tourism experience right in the city.

Can you recommend any other local eco-getaways?

There are so many, from luxury eco-lodges to camping. There are ways of combining different sustainable elements to make your own eco-tour. Research before you go on a biking tour where the farmers markets or local crafts markets are. Stay in a B&B and stop into a local museum where the entrance fee is going directly to the community. . . .

I like to think I have a little bit of eco-travel in every week. Going to the farmers market and talking to a farmer about where they live and what they're growing—that's a connection to a place and a person. I walk to work. And when I get into my building I purposely take the stairs because I want my entire trip to be carbon-neutral. We're all traveling all the time, whether it's next door or to another continent, so how do we interact sustainably?

Green Tourism Tips

Christina Cavaliere says she became a believer in eco-tourism after seeing how changing her behavior and living a more sustainable lifestyle—and witnessing others do so—forged a connection with places and people. Here, she offers tips on making traveling more sustainable.

- Buy and spend local. Stay at a B&B and use local buses, car rental agencies and restaurants. Hire and employ local guides.

- Bring biodegradable soap.

- Don't cover yourself in chemical bug repellent and sunscreens, then jump into a pristine waterway.

- Bring home your trash. Many areas, especially in developing countries, don't have recycling facilities.

- Use refillable water bottles. You can bring your own filter.

- Make sure the lights and air conditioning are off when you leave your hotel room.

- Learn a few words of the local language, an important part of preserving culture.

- Be aware of local conventions and respect them.

- Ask permission before you enter a holy place or if you see a ceremony going on, because often privacy is lost when tourism comes to a community.

- Be sensitive to when, where and how you're taking pictures.

- Respect natural areas. Never touch or harass animals, and stay on designated trails and paths. A lot of endemic and rare plants can be permanently damaged by one step.

- Pay entrance fees to parks and protected areas to help support conservation.

- Pay a fair price for handicrafts and other goods. Try to buy from the individual artisan, and don't buy crafts made from endangered species.

12

Ecotourism Can Harm the Environment

Eric Jaffe

Eric Jaffe is a science writer.

Although it is designed to be an ecologically responsible model of travel, studies show that ecotourism may actually harm the wildlife and natural environments it seeks to protect. Ecotourism is a valuable source of funds for environmental protection and a tool for public education, but the presence of tourists in remote, uninhabited areas causes harm in several ways. Not only do tourists litter and pollute, human disturbance also affects animal behavior and breeding patterns, as seen in the dwindling population of penguins on the Chilean island of Damas. Additionally, ecotourism programs may successfully protect one species, but at the displacement and cost of another. Consequently, further research into the extent of ecotourism's impacts must be done before it can be truly championed.

The island of Damas is a half-hour boat ride from the Chilean coast. On the island, it's dry and rocky. The Humboldt penguins that live there have no ice slopes to slide down in their blacktie apparel. Instead, these desert penguins seek out caves to shade their eggs from the sun. If they can't find a spot beneath a boulder, they may burrow into seabird dung. Sometimes, they nest inside a cactus.

To see these penguins, visitors usually begin in La Serena, Chile. They drive 40 miles north on a main highway and then

Eric Jaffe, "Good Gone Wild: Sometimes, Ecotourism Hurts What it Sets Out to Help," *Science News*, vol. 170, 2006, pp. 218–221. Copyright © 2006 Science Service, Inc. Republished with permission of Science Service, Inc., conveyed through Copyright Clearance Center, Inc.

cut toward the coast on a gravel road that leads to the fishing village of Punta de Choros. Local fishermen there charge a fee to guide the tourists to Damas by boat. On the island, people are free to walk into the caves where the penguins live. Anyone can watch a mother brooding an egg and snap a picture with a flash camera or a mobile phone.

What began in the early 1990s as a place with a few hundred curious visitors has now become a tourism destination that attracts 10,000 penguin peepers a year. Damas provides an example of ecotourism, defined as the practice of visiting sites where exotic landscapes and rare animals are the main attractions. Ideally, ecotourists learn about the habitats that they visit, provide donations to conserve them, and generate income for host communities.

Since this model of tourism emerged some 25 years ago, many special-interest sites, like Damas, have experienced hikes in visitation. Often, ecotourism is a wild success. The United Nations even billed 2002 the "International Year of Ecotourism."

There's been a glib ... championing of ecotourism, that it's a win-win situation.

A More Complicated Picture

But several recent studies show a more complicated picture of the impact of ecotourism, a practice that remains largely unregulated. The increased crowds lead to population changes in some animals, such as the Humboldt penguin and, some 4,000 miles away in the Bahamas, the Allen Cays rock iguana. A mounting garbage problem caused by over-visitation by turtle viewers threatens the beaches of Tortuguero in Costa Rica. People who live near Ghana's Kakum National Park have lost access to the forest's resources and now suffer high rates of unemployment.

"There comes a time when you have so much interference through ecotourism that you affect the thing you're trying to protect," says Robert E. Hueter of the Mote Marine Laboratory in Sarasota, Fla., who studies ecotourism's impact on whale sharks. Ecotourism's benefits to conservation and public education are considerable, he says, but the downsides may take a long time to recognize.

"I think there's been a glib . . . championing of ecotourism, that it's a win-win situation," says Martha Honey, executive director of the Center on Ecotourism and Sustainable Development in Washington, D.C. But by studying how animals, environments, and cultures respond to ecotourism, "we can set up systems that aren't having adverse impacts," she says.

Flight of the Penguins

Ursula Ellenberg decided to study how human disturbance affects the Humboldt penguins when she was quietly counting their population, but not quietly enough. While she was looking through binoculars from a cliff about 150 meters away, the penguins began racing in all directions. One of the penguins had spotted Ellenberg, despite her unobtrusive perch. If a cautious researcher can spark such a reaction, she thought, how would the penguins react to a gaggle of shutter-happy tourists?

To study the effects of human-Humboldt interaction, Ellenberg and her colleagues measured the breeding success of penguins on the islands of Damas, Choros, and Chanaral, which together make up the Humboldt Penguin National Reserve. The island cluster serves as a good point of comparison: Damas receives 10,000 annual visitors, but Choros and Chanaral are much less accessible from the mainland and attract only 1,000 and 100 tourists a year, respectively.

Ellenberg's team was the first to study these penguin populations. The researchers monitored eggs and chicks on each island for 5 months after the penguin mothers laid the eggs. If a nest is abandoned during this period, the chicks usually die. Penguins have many chances to breed during their 20-year life spans, and they would sooner abandon a nest than risk personal harm—say, from an approaching human.

In 2003, the only year that Ellenberg's group studied Chanaral, the penguins there bred an average of 1.34 chicks. On Choros, the average was just below one chick in both 2002 and 2003. But on Damas, female penguins produced, on average, a little less than half a chick in 2002, and the birthrate dipped well below a quarter of a chick in 2003, Ellenberg's team reports online and in the November Biological Conservation.

"It's surprising, when you have islands at such close proximity, that you'd already get a difference," says Ellenberg, a biologist at the University of Otago in New Zealand. "They should do similarly well."

Working in the Bahamas, John Iverson of Earlham College in Richmond, Ind., has discovered similarly detrimental effects of human presence on Allen Cays rock iguanas, an endangered species.

When Iverson began studying these animals 25 years ago [in 1979], ecotourism was just under way. At that point, male iguanas outnumbered females two to one. Historically, fishermen had captured iguanas to sell or eat, and female iguanas were easier to trap because they guard their nests rather than flee an intruder. Iverson and Geoffrey Smith of Denison University in Granville, Ohio, propose in an upcoming Canadian Journal of Zoology that poachers created the observed gender imbalance.

Enter ecotourism. As island management increased protection of its main attraction, poaching declined. The balance of the sexes was restored remarkably quickly. Iverson and Smith found that the increased survival of females that came with the end of poaching wasn't the whole story. Male iguana numbers declined as ecotourism increased, they say.

As part of the study, Iverson and Smith in 2000 tagged the largest male iguanas in two ecotourism areas. At one site, the number of tagged iguanas fell from 30 to 9 by 2005. Using death rates calculated from the previous 20 years, the researchers had predicted that 16 would survive. At the other site, the researchers found none of the 17 tagged iguanas in 2005, though they had expected 9 animals to remain.

Part of the problem, the researchers argue, is that the males tend to be aggressive and interact more with human visitors than females do. Some of the 54,000 people who visit the area each year feed the iguanas hazardous material such as spoiled food or Styrofoam, which can kill them.

Ecotourism may sometimes rescue some animals at the expense of others.

But Iverson and Smith found some of the missing males at nearby islets that iguanas couldn't have reached themselves. This displacement led the researchers to suspect that ecotourism guides had removed many of the large, aggressive male iguanas from the most visited sites.

Moving the iguanas could have ecological ramifications, Iverson says. For example, some of the displaced iguanas were found at sites that are home to an endangered species of seabirds called Audubon's shearwaters. Because the iguanas and the birds require similar nesting territories, the iguanas might crowd out the shearwaters, he says.

In other words, ecotourism may sometimes rescue some animals at the expense of others.

Waste of Space

Visitors travel 3 to 5 hours by boat to reach the beaches of Costa Rica's Tortuguero National Park—home to hawksbill, green, and leatherback turtles. Since the early 1990s, park officials and conservationists have gone to great lengths to protect these rare animals. The money that tourists pay to watch the turtles nest goes to safeguard the species.

But preservation has taken priority over solving a growing waste-management problem that threatens the environment's well-being and, ultimately the turtles' health, says Zoe Meletis of Duke University's Marine Laboratory in Beaufort, N.C. Since Meletis began going to Tortuguero in 2002, the number of tourists has shot from 35,000 to 87,000 a year. And while tourists don't directly harm the turtles, they leave trash such as water bottles and snack wrappers in Tortuguero, which lacks an adequate waste-processing center.

The local government doesn't take responsibility for clearing much of the trash, says Meletis, and boat drivers scoff at transporting waste when they can make more money carrying passengers. Many villagers resort to burning garbage, releasing hazardous compounds into the air. Burying the accumulating waste isn't an option, because refuse contaminates the underground water supply used by local villagers, and waste buried on the beach is re-exposed by ocean waves, creating a hazard for the turtles.

"It's a classic example of ecotourism as a double-edged sword" says Meletis. The same things that draw people to Tortuguero—its isolation and wildlife—make it difficult to manage as a high-volume tourist destination. "It raises a lot of money for turtle conservation," she says. "But some important negative impacts aren't getting the attention they deserve."

When ecotourism in an area grows, the site becomes vulnerable to the same problems, such as sewage maintenance, that come with mass tourism, says John Davenport of University College Cork in Ireland. In the March Estuarine, Coastal and Shelf Science, he reviewed ecotourism's impact on coastal destinations.

Even for activities that aren't usually destructive, a high volume of tourists can create a problem, he says. Such is the case with scuba diving—traditionally a well-managed, environmentally friendly sport. Throughout the world, researchers have seen a link between dive traffic and coral damage, Davenport says. Divers knock into corals or stir up silt that suffocates the reefs, which regenerate slowly.

When divers add an underwater camera to already cumbersome scuba gear—a juggling act that Davenport compares with "driving while having a shave and a smoke"—the damage becomes worse. In Sodwana Bay in South Africa, divers who took underwater photographs damaged reefs by bumping into them on average, during 9 out of 10 dives, whereas divers who didn't take pictures caused such damage in just 1 out of every 6 dives, he reports.

"Since you've got a million new scuba divers [around the world] each year, it's going to be an uphill battle," Davenport says.

Ghost Rainforest

At Kakum National Park in Ghana, the mission to protect the rainforest and its diverse wildlife, while opening the area to tourism, has been successful. Tropical evergreens, endangered forest elephants and bongo antelopes, and some 600 species of butterflies have been preserved, and visitors can experience a bird's-eye glimpse of the forest from a unique canopy walk—a hanging bridge connected at the tops of tall trees.

But the people who live around the park have endured "untold hardships" so that conservation can thrive, says Seth Appiah-Opoku of the University of Alabama in Tuscaloosa, who wrote about their plight in the African Geographical Review in 2004 and who continues to study the area.

After interviewing residents of 100 households in four villages surrounding Kakum, Appiah-Opoku found that the local population had relied heavily on the rainforest: on trees to build homes, on herbs for traditional medicine, and on some animals and plants for food. But once the park opened to the public in 1994, the park's resources became off-limits for these uses.

The restriction has effectively eliminated hunting as a native occupation. In turn, the forest-elephant population has increased, which is bad news for the majority of villagers, who are farmers. The elephants have ravaged roughly 7,800 acres of farmland since the park opened, Appiah-Opoku reports, but killing the animals, even in defense of personal territory, is illegal.

Overall, the unemployment rate has skyrocketed from 3 percent to 27 percent since 1994, and many of the villages are "ghost towns," Appiah-Opoku says. He adds that Kakum National Park officials have confirmed his observations.

"Ecotourism very often is in direct conflict with host communities for its markets and resources," he says. "In a place like this, there should have been an agreement that part of the money would go into the [village] economy, that some of the people would be employed in the park."

We're asking too much from the so-called idea of ecotourism.

But even when local inhabitants participate in the planning, the arrangements often go awry, argues Sanjay Nepal of the University of Texas A&M in College Station. He reports on the cultural impacts of ecotourism in Taiwan in an upcoming *Tourism Management*. If members of the native population don't reap profits from ecotourism, they may focus on their diminished opportunity to harvest the natural resources they had access to in the past, says Nepal.

"One of the things I've lately begun to think is we're asking too much from the so-called idea of ecotourism," he says. "Trying to find a balance between the social, economic, and environmental elements—it's ambitious and it's complex."

The key to this balance is more research, says Honey. As scientists study ecotourism's impacts, new understandings "need to be fed back into the industry, to educate what is acceptable behavior," she says. "There needs to be a closer alliance between hard science and the tourism industry."

Currently, good research on ecotourism is difficult to find, says Davenport. Most destinations weren't studied before ecotourism began, making before-and-after comparisons difficult. Moreover, many governments are reluctant to provide funding for investigations because they profit from ecotourism.

Perhaps the major barrier is the working assumption that ecotourism, with the conservation funds it raises, must be better than typical mass tourism. Says Hueter, "My concern is, that's where the analysis ends, and only in rare cases do [researchers] look deeper."

In the case of the Humboldt penguins, a lack of research led to improper viewing guidelines, says Ellenberg. The Humboldt reserve based its rules for approaching penguins on a related South American species called the Magellanic penguin, which is far less sensitive to human disturbance.

Now, only a few dozen penguins reside on Damas, says Ellenberg. Local fishermen estimate that three times as many lived there before ecotourism began. As today's small population slips further, tourists will head to the nearby islands.

If the guidelines aren't changed quickly, the Humboldt penguins—and ecotourism on Damas and then the other islands—will be gone, says Ellenberg. "And once they're gone, that's it."

13

Volunteer Tourism Has a Positive Impact

Thomas P. Farley

Thomas P. Farley is an author and an editor at Town & Country, *a lifestyle magazine.*

In volunteer tourism, travelers embark on organized trips to impoverished areas around the world and help local communities through hands-on humanitarian efforts, from building homes for poverty-stricken families, to providing basic health care, to teaching English to children. Volunteer tourists may not have the power to change the world, but they make perceptible, real differences in the lives of those less fortunate. These programs offer people ways to get directly involved with humanitarian efforts—and truly connect with cultures and communities—that are more rewarding and beneficial than simply writing checks.

[Since 2001] I've left behind the trappings of Manhattan to spend a week each summer recharging in Mexico. It's not what you think. Mine are not quiet sojourns on the beaches of Cabo. Nor am I painting the town *rojo* in Cancun. Rather, thirty-one others and I—twenty teenagers and a dozen adults—build homes for impoverished families. We start our days far earlier than should be allowed for anyone on vacation, passing and piling cinder blocks, digging foundations and mixing concrete. By late afternoon, having toiled in temperatures that flirt with 100 degrees, we scrub sand, dirt and cement from our bodies in trickling showers with stopped-up drains. We retire a few hours after nightfall, collapsing on army cots or in bunk beds. Not surprisingly, most of us return to the U.S. exhausted, eager for a "real" shower and in need of several good nights' sleep. Friends will ask me, "You call that a *vacation*?" In all honesty, I have to reply that my body never thinks so, but mentally and spiritually, I always feel as though I've been gone for months.

My first time south of the border was in 2001, when I traveled on the initial Mexico expedition made by the Church of the Presentation, a socially responsive Roman Catholic congregation in northern New Jersey. (In addition to the Mexico project, Presentation is involved in regular medical missions to Haiti and runs many other outreach programs.) Since that inaugural trip, the church has made the excursion an annual event, and I've taken an active role in helping to plan the journeys.

A Life That Is Rich

Presentation has come to the aid of the people in encampments on the outskirts of the communities of Reynosa and Miguel Aleman. Both places are shockingly poor yet mere miles from Wal-Marts, Whataburgers and other bastions of consumption over the border in south-central Texas. We typically build two homes, toiling side by side with the men, women and children who will soon reside in them. To qualify for a house, these families must first assist in the construction of shelter for others. When the day finally arrives that their own abode is complete, the families transfer their threadbare possessions from a wood shanty into their new cinder-block structure, which is barely larger than a one-car garage. The windows are glassless. There's no running water or electricity. The women of the house cook over an open fire or on a gas-powered stove. But these families, poverty-stricken though they are, live a life that is rich in many ways. With Mexican blankets, drawings by their children and the smells of freshly made fajitas, the owners turn these spartan concrete structures into love-filled homes. In the process, they've taught me a lifetime's worth of lessons about being thankful for the blessings I have in my own life.

As much as I look forward to these Mexico missions, I never intended for them to become the material for an article. I've also grappled with how a tale so gritty could coexist with the beautiful stories that are the hallmark of *Town & Country*. However, the more I spoke with others who have taken vacations like mine, the more I discovered that many went on their first charitable foray as the direct result of reading a magazine or newspaper account on volunteering.

Fortunately, we in the media don't bear sole responsibility for spreading the word. Led by a generation of baby boomers with the time, the money and the drive to give back, an increasing number of world travelers are making trips such as these the cornerstone of their early retirements or their time away from the office.

Lisa Mendelson of Olympia Fields, Illinois, has taken six journeys to Vietnam with World Missions Possible, a group that performs surgery on children and adults who have cleft lips or cleft palettes. "They're both simple procedures," says Mendelson, "yet can make a huge difference in their lives." She vividly recalls a young man who would not let go of a mirror after seeing himself with a corrected lip for the first time. Although Mendelson brings thirty-nine years' experience as a nurse into the field, she says that her group gladly accepts those who lack such skills, because there are always nonmedical tasks to be done.

Vanessa Sandom, a local politician in Hopewell Township, New Jersey, and a former mayor of that town, traveled a lot as a child and wanted to expose her sons, Alex and Ben (ages fifteen and thirteen), to the world while they were still young. "I'm hoping that they will grow to be more compassionate human beings, not afraid of differences," she says. Together, mother and sons have taken volunteer trips to Ecuador, the Cook Islands and Costa Rica.

"I'll never forget washing my hair on my hands and knees over a bucket," says Carolyn Ladd of Seattle, a former Miss Oregon and currently an attorney for Boeing. "I thought: What am I doing here?" Still, she wouldn't have traded her experience teaching English to children in Ghana for anything. Steve Meadows, an architect and entrepreneur based in Los Angeles, concurs: "A lot of people might rather be on the Spanish Riviera," he told me as he prepared to leave for three months of tsunami relief in Sri Lanka "but I'd be bored there."

Fans of volunteer vacations attest that the bonds they make in local communities take charity to a whole new level.

Other Ways to Get Involved

Excursions such as these (which tend to cost anywhere from several hundred to several thousand dollars, not including airfare) typically require a commitment of one to three weeks. There are also health considerations. Before his trip to Southeast Asia, Meadows says he had twelve shots in fourteen days.

If you decide you are not cut out for this kind of experience, there are always other ways to get involved. Mendelson says that when word got out that the hospital in Vietnam had a shortage of blankets, a group of grandmothers living in Arizona pulled out their knitting needles and quickly whipped up fifteen warm covers to boost the patients' comfort. And in some cases, visiting another nation is possible without even leaving the U.S. John Franke, a senior management consultant based in Washington, D.C., traveled with his wife, Kathleen, to teach schoolchildren in Tuba City, located within the Navajo Nation outside Flagstaff, Arizona. "I felt the days ended too quickly," he says, reflecting on the enjoyment he derived from teaching the youngsters and learning more about their society.

The diversity of international volunteer opportunities now being offered—combined with the chance to get to know people of another culture in ways that are simply not possible on conventional vacations—is what lures many travelers. Rita Johnson, a professor of management and economics at Hamline University, in St. Paul, Minnesota, longed to experience Kenya. Over the course of three trips, each time to assist in the construction of health clinics, she enjoyed living and laughing with her local hosts. Patrice Goldberg of Orange County, California, has donated her time on multiple trips—to Costa Rica, Poland, Ireland, the Cook Islands and Crete. She hopes that the people with whom she works learn about American culture as she learns about theirs.

Fans of volunteer vacations attest that the bonds they make in local communities take charity to a whole new level. "I could just write a check," says Meadows, "but I'd much rather have direct involvement." An admitted recipient of once-a-week manicures and once-a-month pedicures, Ladd says she returned to Seattle "skinny, dirty, hungry and filthy." But she's quick to add, "This is the most important, valuable work I do."

A Tangible Difference

By the end of their trips, most participants say they have received far more from their experiences than they have put in. And the uncanny thing about volunteer vacations is that once you have taken one, you will most certainly sign up for another. Goldberg has become a team leader for the outings she goes on. One of the teenagers with whom I've traveled to Mexico is now at Virginia's College of William & Mary and has initiated trips for her undergraduate peers; another has become an organizer for the National Student Campaign Against Hunger and Homelessness and is a cochair of a social-justice group at Loyola College, in Baltimore. Debbie Wissel of Manhattan, who made her first trip to Nicaragua with Bridges to Community while she was a sophomore in high school, has returned five times and now serves on that group's board. Doing good, it turns out, can be surprisingly addictive.

Before long, veterans of these trips start looking at the material world in different ways. Bess Kargman, a recent college graduate who is planning a career in the music industry, recalls giving an apple to a little girl in South Africa. Kargman fully expected the girl to gobble it down the moment it was in her hands. Instead, the youngster walked around and shared it with her friends, each one taking a microscopic bite. Even more startling was the reaction Kargman encountered when she offered her empty water bottle to an impoverished Ethiopian woman. "She started crying because she finally had something to put water in besides a plastic bag with a hole in it."

Volunteers operate under no illusion that they can fix the problems of the world. But they do feel good knowing that they have worked with the residents of one small corner of the globe to make a tangible difference. "You have to come back changed," says Rita Johnson, "or you're not alive."

14

Volunteer Tourism May Not Have a Lasting Positive Impact

Foreign Policy Magazine

Foreign Policy Magazine *is published by the Carnegie Endowment for International Peace in Washington, D.C. and is the premier, award-winning magazine of global politics, economics, and ideas.*

Participating in volunteer tourism, or traveling abroad to provide charitable services to a poverty-stricken community during the span of a vacation, is a noble gesture, but its impacts may be negligible. Foreign Policy Magazine *dubs volunteer tourism "disaster tourism," stating that it's "traversing the globe to gawk at the aftermath of natural and man-made catastrophes." The following viewpoint provides a list of examples of "voluntourism" vacations that ultimately benefit the travel agencies much more than the locals. Individuals seeking to make a difference in the world, rather than to enhance their resumes, should reconsider volunteering at home.*

Disaster tourism isn't getting sunburned or leaving your travelers checks at home. It's traversing the globe to gawk at the aftermath of natural and man-made catastrophes. In this week's List, Foreign Policy explores the disaster zones that today's intrepid (and voyeuristic) explorers are increasingly making their destinations of choice.

Hurricane Holiday

The place: New Orleans, La.

The tour: Bus tours of neighborhoods ravaged by the 2005 hurricane and its aftermath.

The itinerary: Gray Line New Orleans offers a $35 tour titled, "Hurricane Katrina—America's Worst Catastrophe," which busses tourists from the French Quarter past the Super-dome and Convention Center and into destroyed and still-vacant neighborhoods. The Big Easy–based company Tours by Isabelle takes visitors to the site of levee breaches for $53 a person. New Orleans residents have expressed irritation with the tours, which inch through their neighborhoods as riders snap photos of the devastation and even walk among the debris, but tour officials insist they're providing much-needed public education about the extent of the hurricane's wrath.

Radioactive R & R

The place: The Chernobyl nuclear reactor and surrounding villages, site of the infamous 1986 nuclear meltdown

The tour: Day-trips by van and bus from Kiev, Ukraine

The itinerary: Thousands of visitors each year make the trek to this Soviet time capsule; the villages near Chernobyl—from which more than 100,000 residents fled—have remained largely uninhabited since that fateful day. For a few hundred dollars, visitors receive a change of clothes and shoes, sightsee around the abandoned town of Pripyat, and stop near the "Red Forest" that was created by falling radioactive material. They can also observe Reactor 4 from a "safe" distance of less than half a mile, visit with residents who have returned to the area, and dine on a lunch prepared and delivered from outside the contaminated zone. Visitors even receive their own personal dosimeter to measure radiation in the atmosphere.

A Flood of Tourists

The place: The Southeast Asian region devastated by the 2004 Asian tsunami, including Indonesia, Sri Lanka, and Thailand

The tour: Package trips to tsunami-affected areas that combine R & R with volunteer and reconstruction projects

---

Travelers have continued to flock to the ruined areas, often under the guise of reconstruction tourism.

The itinerary: Because many of the regions hardest hit by the 2004 tsunami depended on tourism, many industry experts worried that the devastation would only be compounded by the lack of future visitors. But to the surprise of many, travelers have continued to flock to the ruined areas, often under the guise of reconstruction tourism. Travel agencies, including Britain's Different Travel, offer package deals that enable tourists to travel to Sri Lanka and southern Thailand to combine beach-hopping and city sightseeing with volunteer work such as rebuilding houses and schools and assisting at local orphanages. In 2005, so many foreign backpackers flocked to Thai islands to assist with the recovery effort that one local organization, Help International Phi Phi, put them to work alongside locals, earning it one of *Time Asia's* Heroes awards.

Volcanic Vacation

The place: Mount St. Helens in southern Washington State

The tour: Climbing the active volcano that blew its top in May 1980

The itinerary: Climbing was again permitted in July 2006, after being suspended for two years due to the volcano's unpredictable activity. Although the volcano regularly spews steam, ash, and volcanic dust, it has settled into what the U.S. Forest Service considers a slow period (though authorities warn climbers that larger eruptions could occur at any time). One of the 10 essential items climbers should carry with them on their journey to the crater? Emergency shelter.

Trip to the Poorhouse

The place: Sprawling slums around Brazilian cities called *favelas*

The tour: Guided tours by foot and car through economic disaster zones, such as the illegal and desperately poor shanty-towns of Rocinha and Vila Canoas in Rio de Janeiro

The itinerary: Local guides usher tourists through Brazil's underbelly, urban neighborhoods where drug gangs reign supreme, offering the social services and justice that the government has neglected to provide. In Rio, where a fifth of the residents live in *favelas* that abut some of the city's richest locales, tourists can visit the homes of *favela* residents, attend locally run schools and medical clinics, and admire the infrastructure projects built by crime barons. To make up for rubbernecking Brazil's worst poverty, tour operators often give a portion of the takings to social projects in the neighborhoods.

Organizations to Contact

The editors have compiled the following list of organizations concerned with the issues debated in this book. The descriptions are derived from materials provided by the organizations. All have publications or information available for interested readers. The list was compiled on the date of publication of the present volume; the information provided here may change. Be aware that many organizations take several weeks or longer to respond to inquiries, so allow as much time as possible.

The Mesoamerican Ecotourism Alliance (MEA)
4076 Crystal Court, Boulder, CO   80304
(800) 682-0584 • fax: (303) 447-0815
e-mail: mark@travelwithmea.org
Web site: www.travelwithmea.org

MEA is an alliance of local organizations committed to the development and promotion of sustainable tourism as a means for supporting conservation efforts in Mesoamerica. MEA operates in Honduras, Belize, Guatemala, El Salvador, Nicaragua, Panama, and Chiapas and Yucatán, Mexico.

OpenmindProjects
1039/3 Keawworawut Road
Amphor Muang, Nong Khai   43000
   Thailand
Web site: www.openmindprojects.org

OpenmindProjects is a private aid organization focused on environment projects and regards international volunteers as a highly valuable source of support. OpenmindProjects arranges volunteer projects in Thailand, Cambodia, Nepal, and Laos.

The International Ecotourism Society (TIES)
1333 H St, NW, Suite 300E, Washington, DC   20005
(202) 347-9203 • fax: (202) 789-7279

e-mail: info@ecotourism.org
Web site: www.ecotourism.org

Established in 1990, TIES is the oldest and largest ecotourism nonprofit organization in the world. It promotes responsible travel to natural areas that conserve the environment and improve the well-being of local people by creating an international network of individuals, institutions, and the tourism industry; educating tourists and tourism professionals; and influencing the tourism industry, public institutions, and donors to integrate the principles of ecotourism into their operations and policies.

Travel Industry Association (TIA)
1100 New York Avenue, NW Suite 450
Washington, DC   20005-3934
(202) 408-8422 • fax (202) 408-1255
e-mail: feedback@tia.org
Web site: www.tia.org

TIA is a nonprofit trade organization that represents the U.S. travel industry. TIA promotes increased travel to and within the United States as well as serving as an advocate with the U.S. government to ease travel procedures. The association's travel research offers statistics and analyses on the size and economic impact of the industry as well as in marketing and other areas.

United Nations Environment Programme (UNEP)
Division of Technology, Industry, and Economics
    Tourism Programme
Paris, Cedex 09 75441
    France
+33 1 4437 1450 • fax: +33 1 4437 1474
e-mail: tourism@unep.fr
Web site: www.unep.fr/scp/tourism

UNEP tourism program is a branch established by the United Nations that addresses the social, economic, and environmental issues of tourism. Its mission is to mainstream sustainability into tourism development by demonstrating the economic, environmental, and socio-cultural benefits of sustainable tourism.

VolunTourism
717 Third Avenue, Chula Vista, CA   91910
(619) 434-6230 • fax: (619) 426-6664
vt@voluntourism.org
Web site: www.voluntourism.org

VolunTourism is an organization that educates travelers about volunteer tourism and helps develop volunteer tourism programs with host destinations, operators, suppliers, nonprofits, and corporations. It provides a weekly webcast and quarterly newsletter on issues affecting volunteer tourism.

World Tourism Organization (UNWTO/OMT)
Capitán Haya 42, Madrid   28020
    Spain
+34 91 567 81 00 • fax +34 91 571 37 33
e-mail: omt@unwto.org
Web site: www.unwto.org

UNWTO/OMT is a specialized agency of the United Nations and the leading international organization in the field of tourism. It serves as a global forum for tourism policy issues and a practical source of tourism know-how. It promotes the development of responsible, sustainable, and universally accessible tourism, paying particular attention to the interests of developing countries.

Bibliography

Books

Milica Z. Bookman and Karla R. Bookman	*Medical Tourism in Developing Countries.* New York, NY: Palgrave Macmillan, 2007.
Peter Burns and Marina Novelli, eds.	*Tourism and Mobilities: Local-Global Connections.* Cambridge, MA: CABI, 2008.
Jeremy Buultjens and Don Fuller	*Striving for Sustainability: Case Studies in Indigenous Tourism.* Lismore, Australia: Southern Cross University Press, 2007.
Julia O'Connell Davidson	*Children in the Global Sex Trade.* Cambridge, MA: Polity, 2005.
David A. Fennell	*Ecotourism: An Introduction,* 2nd ed. New York, NY: Routledge, 2003.
C. Michael Hall and Allan M. Williams	*Tourism and Innovation.* New York, NY: Routledge, 2008.
Mason R. McWatters	*Residential Tourism: (De)constructing Paradise.* Buffalo, NY: Channel View Publications, 2008.
Greg Richards, ed.	*Cultural Tourism: Global and Local Perspectives.* New York, NY: Haworth Hospitality Press, 2007.

Melanie K. Smith, *Tourism, Culture, and Regeneration.*
ed. Cambridge, MA: CABI, 2007.

Periodicals

Julie Bindel "Tourism Built on Abuse," *Guardian*, December 18, 2007.

David Carpenter "'Voluntourism' Vacations Taking Off," *Washington Post*, March 29, 2007.

Jeffrey Fleishman and Noha El-Hennawy "In Egypt, Tourism and Islam Live Uneasily Side-by-Side," *Los Angeles Times*, October 7, 2007.

Leslie Garrett "The Sex Tourism Dilemma: Most Onlookers Do Nothing," *Toronto Star*, January 17, 2008.

Lauren Goering "For Big Surgery, Delhi Is Dealing; Medical Tourism Soars as Americans Seek Major Savings on Health Care in Hospitals Abroad," *Chicago Tribune*, March 28, 2008.

Jodi Helmer "Understanding Ecoadventures: Yes, You Can Enjoy the Environment and Protect It at the Same Time," *Curve*, November 2007.

Mary Jordan "Seeking Answers with Field Trips in Faith," *Washington Post*, June 25, 2007.

Charles Levinson "Terror Threat Not Halting Tourism," *USA Today*, August 1, 2005.

Economist	"A New Itinerary—Travel and Tourism," *Economist* (US), May 17, 2008.
The Age	"Older White Women Join Kenya's Sex Tourists," *The Age*, November 26, 2007.
David Sherwood	"Costa Rica Sees Tourism's Environmental Dark Side," *Christian Science Monitor*, April 17, 2008.
Cathy Booth Thomas	"The Space Cowboys," *Time*, February 22, 2007.
Bonnie Tsui	"Ecotourism: Traveling the World to Help Save It," *New York Times*, December 17, 2006.
Eric Weiner	"Slum Visits: Tourism or Voyeurism?" *International Herald-Tribune*, March 12, 2008.
Melanie Wells	"The Joy of a Staycation," *Wall Street Journal*, May 23, 2008.

Index

A

Aboriginal communities (Australia), 53

Airline emissions, 16, 24, 65–66

Allen Cays rock iguanas, 83–84

Alternative fuels, search for, 15–16

Anangu indigenous culture (Australia), 53

Angkor Temples, 71

Anti-apartheid movement, 53

Arup Group (United Kingdom), 10

Ashton Hayes village (northern England) energy movement, 20–21

Australia
attempts at prostitution de-criminalization, 57–58
sex tourism to Cambodia, 58

Automobile Club of America (AAA), 21

B

Baumgarten, Jean Claude (WTTC president), 12, 14

Biodiversity initiatives, 50–52

Bourbon Street (New Orleans), 72

Branson, Richard, 7, 15–16

"Breaking Barriers and Managing Growth" theme (Global Travel and Tourism Summit), 12

Bridges to Community, 94

British Airways Sustainable Business Unit, 27

British Broadcasting Corporation (BBC), 48

Brothels
in Australia, 57–58
in Cambodia, 58
See also Prostitution; Sex trafficking problem

Brundtland Report, 53

Burnham, Bonnie (WMF president), 71

C

Cable News Network (CNN), 48

Cambodia, sex crimes against minors, 58

Car rental industry, 15

Carbon
impact on global warming, 15
offsetting of, 26–27
zero emissions goal, 19

Carbon Fund (nonprofit organization), 15

Cavaliere, Christina, 75–79

Cayapas indigenous community (Ecuador), 44–45

Center on Ecotourism and Sustainable Development (Washington, DC), 82

Ceremonies of indigenous cultures, 51–52

Children, sexual slavery of, 56–59

Chilling system, investment in, 19–20

Church of the Presentation (New Jersey), 90

The City Builders (Fainstein), 46

Clarke, Jeff (CEO of Travelport), 14–15

Climate Care, 26

ecotourism's negative impact
on, 50–52
Karen of Thailand, 51
Maasai of Kenya and Tanza-
nia, 51
Maori of New Zealand, 53
Mayans of South America, 45,
51
supportive legislation, 52, 55
tourism's helping of, 43–47
tourism's threatening of,
48–55
tribal unity concept, 52–53
See also Declaration of the
Rights of Indigenous
Peoples; Russell Tribunal;
United Nations, Permanent
Forum on Indigenous Issues;
World Council of Indigenous
Peoples
Industrial tourism, 49
InterContinental Bora Bora Re-
sort, 18–19
InterContinental Hotels Group
(HIG), 13
International Ecotourism Society
(TIES), 75–76
International Panel on Climate
Change (IPCC), 24
International Space Station, 7
Iraq (country) as endangered
world site, 72
Iverson, John, 83–84

J

Jaffe, Eric, 80–88
Johnston, Alison, 48–55
Jones Lang LaSalle Hotels, 16–17

K

Kaitiakitanga (guardianship) principle of Maori, 53

Kakum National Park (ghost
rainforest), Ghana, 86–87
Karen indigenous culture of Thailand, 51
Kaumaitotoya, Banuve, 66

L

Ladd, Carolyn, 92
Law Reform Commission
(Australia), 57
Leeds Metropolitan University
(Great Britain), 43
Legalization of prostitution, at-
tempts at, 57–58
Leisure tourism, 12
Lijiang (China) World Heritage
site, 45, 46
Lindblad Expeditions, 72
Lipman, Geoffrey, 65, 66
Luang Prahang (Laos) World
Heritage site, 45
Luebkeman, Chris, 10–11, 15, 20
Luzadder, Dan, 10–22
Lynx rocketplane (XCOR
Aerospace), 7–8

M

Maasai indigenous culture, 51
Mabuza, Jabulani (CEO, Tsogo
Sun Holdings), 17
Machu Picchu (Peru), 52, 70
Maori indigenous culture (New
Zealand), 53
Margolis, Mac, 69–74
Marriott International Hotels, 16
Mayan indigenous community, 45,
51
McMenamin, Bernadette, 59
Meadows, Steve, 92
Meletis, Zoe, 85

Mendelson, Lisa, 91

Mexico City's pre-Columbian ruins, 73

Mexico missions. *See* Volunteer tourism

Mote Marine Laboratory, 82

N

National Student Campaign Against Hunger and Homelessness, 93–94

Natural Air (airline), 15

Natural Habitat organization, 73

Neave, Marcia, 57

Negative impacts of tourism industry

air pollution, 24

climate change, 25–26

culture loss, 49

economic dependence of local community, 41

environmental harm, 80–88

export leakage, 39

import leakage, 38–39

on indigenous culture, 50–52

infrastructure cost, 40

local economic crises, 41–42

loss of money for locals, 25

price increases, 40–41

seasonality of jobs, 41

See also Industrial tourism

New Orleans hurricane disaster, 70

New Zealand tourism strategy, 53

O

"Open aviation area" between US/ European Union, 35–36

"Open-air brothel" in Australia, 57

Orbitz Web travel service, 14

P

Penguins of Damas island, 80–83, 88

Prostitution, 56–59

R

Ringbeck, Jurgen, 29–36

Rosenthal, Elisabeth, 64–68

Russell Tribunal (Europe), 52–53

Rutan, Burt, 8

S

Sacred sites, negative impact of ecotourism, 51–52

Sandom, Vanessa, 91

Sex trafficking problem

abduction of children/women, 56–57

prostitution, attempts at legalization, 57–58

Sexually transmitted diseases (STDs), 57–58

Shivdasani, Sonu (CEO, Six Senses Resorts and Spas), 19

Six Senses Resorts and Spas (Thailand, Maldives, Vietnam), 19

The Snows of Kilimanjaro (Hemingway), 69–70

Souvenirs and indigenous culture, 45

Soyuz TM-32 manned space supply mission, 7

Space tourism, 7–9

SpaceShipOne (Virgin Galactic), 7, 8

Stonehenge (England), 70

Stover, Anne, 56–59

Summit. *See* Global Travel and Tourism Summit (of WTTC)
Sustainable tourism, 18, 50

T

Taj Mahal, 71
Temples of Luxor, 70
Terrorism, impact on tourism, 60–63
Thalasso Spa, 18
Three Gorges hydroelectric dam (China), 73–74
Timbuktu adobe mosques, 72
Tito, Dennis, 7
Tortuguero National Park (Costa Rica), 84–86
Tower of London, 72
Travel and tourism (T&T) industry
  benefits vs. negative impact, 27
  contribution to exploitation of children/women, 56–59
  drivers of competitiveness of, 31–33
  ease of travel, 70
  economic growth from, 29–36
  effect of climate change on, 64–68
  evaluation/ranking of (international), 30–31
  growth of environmental awareness, 12–13
  indigenous culture helped by, 43–47
  indigenous culture threatened by, 48–55
  locals' loss of dollars, 25
  need for cleansing of "isms," 55
  as new source of wealth, 34–35
  steps of improvement, 33–34

sustainable, talks about, 18
world landmarks threatened by, 69–74
  See also Ecotourism; Industrial tourism; Sustainable tourism; Volunteer tourism
Travel and Tourism Competitiveness Report 2007 (Booz Allen Hamilton), 29, 35
Travel tips for responsible travel, 28
Travel Weekly magazine, 12, 14
Tree planting in Costa Rica, 16
Tribal unity concept, 52–53
Tsogo Sun Holdings, 17
T&T industry. See travel and tourism (T&T) industry

U

Uluru sacred site (Australia), 52, 53
United Nations (UN)
  "Climate Change and Tourism" conference, 65
  Committee on Decolonization, 53
  Convention on Biological Diversity, 53–55
  Declaration of the Rights of Indigenous Peoples, 55
  Permanent Forum on Indigenous Issues, 49
  World Tourism Organization, 23, 65, 68
United Nations Educational, Scientific, and Cultural Organization (UNESCO), 74
United Nations Foundation, 17
United Nations University, 72
United Nations World Travel Organization (UNWTO), 30, 32
Unsustainability of tourism, 70–72

110